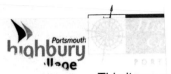

LITERACY AND PRE-SCHOOL
the roles of teachers and parents

LITERACY IN THE PRE-SCHOOL
the roles of teachers and parents

Bronwyn Reynolds

Trentham Books

LITERACY IN THE PRE-SCHOOL: THE ROLES OF TEACHERS AND PARENTS

First published in 1997 by Trentham Books Limited

Trentham Books Limited
Westview House
734 London Road
Oakhill
Stoke on Trent
Staffordshire
England ST4 5NP

British Cataloguing in Publication Data
A catalogue record for this book is available from the British Library
ISBN: 1 85856 075 6

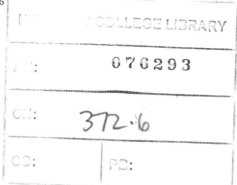

Designed and typeset by Trentham Print Design Ltd., Chester
and printed in Great Britain by Henry Ling Ltd., Dorset

Contents

Acknowledgements

This publication includes many voices and my debts are numerous. The greatest is to my husband John and children Kieran, Carla and Julian, for their endless support.

A special thank you also to all the staff at the Early Learning Centre, particularly Annette MacDonald and Julie Nihill, for their total commitment towards the care and education of young children.

I would further like to thank Professor Bridie Raban for her inspiration and guidance, and for making this book a dream come true.

This book however, is dedicated to Eltham College, especially to the children and families associated with the Early Learning Centre. I owe a debt of gratitude particularly to all the young children in my 1995 and 1996 groups, for giving me valuable insights into how pre-school age children learn literacy.

My thanks also extend to the parents for permission to publish the photographs, letters and the children's work. This documentation helped me not only to travel along the children's literacy learning pathways but to reflect on and revisit my work often.

A final thank you to Trentham Books for publishing this work. The recognition that literacy begins in the very early years and the implications of this notion for teachers and parents of young children will, I hope, enlighten us forever.

Foreword

It takes great courage for a successful and highly acclaimed professional to re-evaluate and plan to change their practice. Yet this is what Bronwyn Reynolds has done and this book is an account of that experience from her point of view. She captures well the dilemma of so many pre-school teachers:

> What is my role in children's learning?
> When should I intervene?
> When should I step back?
> Should I teach directly, or not at all?
> Should support and facilitating be enough?
> What is the difference?
> What does my training tell me?
> What does my experience of working with children suggest?

These were all nagging questions for Bronwyn. She was further fuelled by an increasing, legitimate demand from her articulate group of parents who wanted to know all about their children learning to read and write, and what they should do. The traditional responses of:

> Wait until they start school.
> There isn't any need to pressure them at this age.

> Don't do anything because it might confuse them when they get to school.

These are familiar conversations we have all had with parents.

But, as always, it was the children who pushed the ideas forward. They asked constantly:

How do I write my name? What does that say?
Can you help me write my present list?
I want to write to my friend I met on holiday.
Show me how to do that there? (pointing to writing).

They wanted their names on their pictures, they loved listening to stories and joining in. Is that where literacy learning stops in the pre-school? Bronwyn decided that's where support for literacy learning starts.

She considered her current practice and reviewed her program, its activities and resources and the room she shared with the children. She reviewed all this pragmatically and critically. She decided to reflect her own fascination with books and literacy into her Centre generally through rewriting the policy documentation and more particularly in her room where print would accompany all objects and activities in a relevant and interesting way. This fundamental inclusion of literacy would involve the children and their views would be sought at every opportunity.

Importantly, areas of the room would become dedicated to reading and to writing. The Once Upon a Time corner became the focus for book displays and browsing. The writing table became a busy office desk with writing equipment: paper, envelopes, pens, pencils, an alphabet frieze, a post box, a telephone and message pad, a computer and mouse (real and home-made).

Once the children's imagination was captured through this new journey towards literacy they soon incorporated reading, books and writing in all their activities in a very matter of fact way. Indeed, we soon discovered that the children dictated the pace of their literacy learning and it was a breathless time keeping up with their demands for reading and writing opportunities.

While we have quantitative data which indicates the magnitude of these children's literacy progress through this pre-school period, we are even more impressed with their literacy development through their first year of formal schooling. Bronwyn says that now it is hard to remember what she used to do, because what she does now with the children all seems so natural.

It is this 'naturalness' of literacy events within her program for these three and four year old children which is at the heart of its success. The account she has written here will inform many colleagues who, like Bronwyn, are ready to move forward in their own work with children. All adults, parents and teachers, have a vital role in children's literacy development at all ages. Here we see that collaborative partnership being developed and sustained.

It is an exciting and rewarding journey and the sense of authenticity which comes from these pages will support many more teachers as they explore their own practice and young children's literacy development.

Professor Bridie Raban
Mooroolbeek Chair of Early Childhood Education
The University of Melbourne, Australia
1997

When are you going to teach my child to read?

As a pre-school teacher for more than twenty years this comment from a parent recently was probably one of the most precious requests I have ever received. Not only did it help me to reflect on my professional development in the pursuit to improve my teaching style, methodology and learning outcomes for the children, but it facilitated my working partnership with the parents.

However, at the beginning I didn't perceive this remark as an enlightenment at all, yet what it did do was to encourage an examination of my role as a teacher. For at this stage I still had an overriding source of anxiety concerning the notion of 'teaching' in my professional role and I found the term inappropriate in the context of my work with young children. I also held a sliding philosophical belief that the teaching of reading was the domain not of the pre-school curriculum but of the school. I still remember quite vividly the cloud of confusion creeping into my thoughts at this time and the questions I kept asking myself. What should I be saying to parents with respect to the children's developing literacy? How can I justify my answers to questions about literacy by only talking about pre-reading and pre-writing skills? What really was my philosophy?

After some thought I decided the best way to work through this reflective process was to look back through some of my written work. Mind you I also had to brain storm in order to put my teaching philosophy into some sort of evolving sequence, so I could see more clearly where I was coming from. It's noteworthy to mention here that Tricia David concurs with a similar focus of ideologies during the decades in her book, *Under Five – Under Educated?* (1990).

The seventies

The starting point takes me back to the early seventies when I first began teaching. It was my first position as a pre-school teacher and I had been asked by the Committee of Management to present a statement about my teaching philosophy. It was indeed a piece of work that I laboured over, especially because I had to articulate my viewpoint. I wrote, 'For most children the pre-school constitutes the first stage in the continuing educational process. The planned program is designed for the children to learn to adjust to a wider and less secure environment than provided for it in the family unit. It is concerned with the social and emotional development of each individual child and the recognition of the value of free play in the development and learning of the young child...' I chose to stop at this point of the report for I believe it emphasised the emotional and social development of the children as the over-arching aim during this period.

The early eighties

At the beginning of this decade I still espoused a child-centred philosophy. Nevertheless there was a subtle difference in emphasis. My aims during this period confirmed a strong focus on the children's language development. It was also at this point in my career that I became consciously aware of questioning my beliefs and pedagogy.

It was this latter concept that really troubled me, for I was only seeing myself, the teacher, as a 'social butterfly'. To be more truthful I knew that I was an enthusiastic and dedicated teacher, but one who was constantly on the move around the room. This nomadic orientation was considered absolutely essential for the control of any inappropriate behaviour. This so-called butterfly approach was also to observe the children's learning through their spontaneous play.

On a more positive note, this style of teaching was all carried out in what I considered to be a carefully planned and pre-structured environment. Yet what really concerned me about my own pedagogy was the fact that I never felt in tune with the children. I considered my communicative style unattached, uninvolved and consequently non-productive towards the children's learning. In other words I never fully interacted with the children to support their learning.

Perhaps you could imagine some of the thought provoking questions that empowered me at this time. Blurring my mind were statements like – The children are not developing in a holistic manner? Some children don't learn simply through free play? Where are the missing links in my teaching presentation? An ominous cloud was forming and my observations at the time suggested that some children were merely being occupied through play, whilst others appeared to be making real contributions to their educational advancement.

The late eighties

Around this time my reflectiveness was more of a constructive criticism towards the traditional type of pre-school program, where the teacher offers a child-centred, prestructured environment based on free play, with little adult intervention. Already a recognition of the need to become a constructive communicator

and a facilitator had become a high priority, because I realised that this approach was the one most conducive to the children's learning. Vygotsky (1962) also illustrates the important role adults have to play in social interactions for the children's learning.

A model of the Sydney Harbour Bridge

I knew what was necessary and I still recall that captivating desire to reach the optimum outcome, that of a triangular partnership between the parent, teacher and child. This period of my teaching saw new pathways opening and developing, and a conscious awareness of me the teacher, becoming more skilled as a reflective practitioner and active listener. I became more accountable for my professional actions and felt more comfortable articulating my teaching philosophy to the parents. Formal interviews were also well established with the parents, not only to discuss their children's progress, but to collaborate on different curriculum developments.

The early nineties

By the early nineteen nineties the haze over my philosophy had lifted somewhat, although several aspects of my program, which I will mention later, still bothered me. With an awareness of certain societal expectations of both myself and the children and a simultaneous recognition of the children's interests and needs, what gradually evolved was a pre-school curriculum which offered cognitive challenge, through both free and guided play and exploration. The need to scaffold the children's learning through cognitive challenge and dialogue became very obvious.

Early 1995

Yet in continually striving to reach a greater teaching optimum I found myself with another missing link. My eager attempts to foster the children's early literacy still phased me. I felt quite inadequate in this area of my partnership with the children and with the parents. I know now that it all stemmed from the traditional idea that the learning of literacy was not part of the pre-school curriculum. You see, in early childhood circles there has always been a code of curricula that suggests the teaching of literacy before school could lead to children being placed under too much pressure, and the children being taught by the wrong methods. As an early childhood educator I was always led to believe that my jurisdiction in this area was confined to the development of the children's pre-reading and pre-writing skills.

However, after this parental request – When are you going to teach my child to read? I began seriously to question several aspects of my profession, namely, my role as an early childhood educator, how children really learn and the importance of parents as educators. This last aspect was a real contradiction for me, because I was telling parents that they are their children's most important teachers, yet I was excluding them from supporting their children's literacy learning. For I was already aware that literacy learning began at a very early stage in a child's development and an amusing example of this still regularly comes to mind. Several years ago a young mother came up to me, excited because her thirteen month old daughter, whilst sitting in the back seat of the car, pointed and called out, 'Mama, Mac, Mac!' 'Yes, it was a MacDonald's sign', her mother said, 'And she clearly wanted a hamburger'. This little anecdote is a good illustration that the learning of literacy doesn't occur in a vacuum. What it highlights is that children learn about literacy in contexts where it is meaningful for them (Goodman, 1986; Hall, 1987).

PART 2

THE BEGINNING

After travelling through my reflections and with the knowledge that literacy doesn't start with formal schooling, I was then presented with a challenging opportunity to explore different ways of generating emergent literacy within the pre-school curriculum. The idea sounded exciting, but the thought of implementing such a program created a great deal of anxiety for me. Where was I to start?

With support and guidance I set out on a journey of reading and indeed discovery about emergent literacy. The work of Clay (1991), David (1990), Ferreiro and Teberosky (1983), Hall (1987), Harste, *et al* (1984), the Goodmans (1982 and 1986) and many others, all contributed to this adventure. These readings highlighted a lack of constructive intervention and a reasonably low focus towards developing the children's emerging literacy within my program. In these days before adult intervention the children had to rely mainly on their own experiences to create contexts for literacy interactions in their play. Few cues or props were available to scaffold their literacy learning.

Redesigning the classroom

One of my first moves was to redesign sections of the play environment for literacy enrichment purposes. This involved minor physical changes, additions, the purchasing of some new

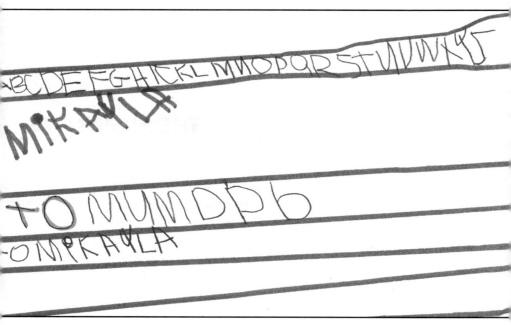

but inexpensive equipment and the making of some props. Already existing were play centres like the library area, home corner, block section and art and craft area, which had been carved away from one another using permanent fixtures and semi-fixed features, such as wooden shelving, screens and tables.

A child's letter to her parents, incorporating the alphabet

Creating a literate environment

It was decided to set up a permanent writing area for the children – but I cannot take much credit for this idea. A boy in the group, called Brent, instigated it before I could put my plan into practice. We were both sitting at the drawing table when suddenly he looked up at me and said, 'How do you write Edward's name?' I suggested that he get the name cards from the shelf near our mat time area, and copy Edward's name. Brent

The Writing Area followed the instructions, found Edward's name and proceeded to copy it. After an excellent attempt at this he said, 'Well then how do you write my brother's name, James?' I spelt out the letters, but he quickly retorted, 'I don't know how to write them. You need to have the A B C up here Bronwyn!' I found a chart and stuck it up on the back of the shelf which divided the block section off from the drawing table.

I then asked Brent if we should make a sign for this area and he said, 'Yeah! We could make it our writing and drawing place'. So a sign was promptly made that read: 'This is our drawing and writing table'.

The position of the writing area was not altered from the original location I had planned. The main reason for leaving it in this prominent position was because it meant easy access to the home corner, block section and the library area. I anticipated

that the close proximity would facilitate movement between the centres and encourage the development of coherent and ongoing play themes. A provision was also made for an abundant supply of paper, pads, bank slips, coloured and black lead pencils, rulers, magazines, alphabet stencils, erasers, sharpeners, clip-boards, staplers, sticky tape, scissors and so forth to be available in this area at all times. Another noticeable addition was the placement of a letter-box on top of a shelf next to the writing area.

Flash cards were placed in the writing area

Flash cards were already an invaluable part of the program. They included the children's printed names and the names and illustrations of songs they had learnt. I added to these sets by making up more flash cards showing numbers, days of the week

Several children engaging in their own story time, using felt pieces

and the children's family names. Instead of keeping the cards for teacher aid purposes during different mat time experiences, I placed them all in the writing area for the children to use as they decided.

In continuing my preparation for an enriched literacy environment I realised was that the library corner only required sprucing up. Because of my abiding passion for books my efforts to create an inviting atmosphere had already included stocking the library shelves with books of many levels and interests, providing comfortable and varied seating arrangements, such as sofas, bean bags, chairs and a small table. Partitions already existed and the location provided not only intimacy but quietness.

Basically any improvements to the library corner meant beautification only. To develop this area into one of tranquillity we placed a fish tank in one of the corners. Posters relating to children's literature were pinned up and appropriate illustrations covered the display boards. A sign announcing 'Our Library Area' was strategically placed and writing eventually accompanied all picture displays. Extra props included magazines, newspapers, comics, a small felt board with story-related felt pieces and provision for taped stories with head-phones.

'Podd' was the children's favourite computer character

Stories and language games on CD ROM also became new acquisitions for the children to use on the computer. They included 'Grandma and Me', 'Little Monster Goes To School', 'Playtime in The Park' and alphabet rhymes. Kids Pix was a

The Puppet area program previously available on the Macintosh. Podd was a favourite character on one of the BBC programs and encouraged the children's literacy development.

In the desire to create a literate environment for the children a felt story-board, a puppet theatre, weather board and calendar all became permanent fixtures, and all were progressively and appropriately labelled and positioned.

The careful locating of these props and charts resulted in easy access and excellent viewing from the mat where the children sat at group time. Relevant labelling and written work were placed above or on these props. Some of the writing read, 'ELC (Early Learning Centre) Calendar', 'Weather Forecast' and 'Today our story is...'

Big book reading

Apart from naming different areas of interest on display boards, some specific labelling relating to the children's birthdays, some writing about particular computer programs and a reasonably large poster of the alphabet displayed above the computer, there was very little print displayed in the room. So I set to work with the children and gradually created a print filled environment. Labels and signs were placed around the room and a large hand-written alphabet was displayed on the back board above the mat time area for prominent viewing. Numerous alphabet charts were also placed on the backs of shelves and on the tables in the writing area. Signs acknowledging the different play centres such as 'Our Home Corner Area', 'Our Block Area', 'Our Painting Area', and 'Our Mat Time Area', were also made and placed in appropriate positions.

The Computer Area

All the changes carried out, however, did involve the children through either spontaneous or formal discussions. They helped in the decision making and contributed some of the props like cookery books for the home corner, a continuous supply of empty grocery boxes and posters. Other items such as utensils, cutlery, plastic fruit, a telephone and directory were already provided in the house-keeping area.

Ready Set Go

Perhaps this section of the process of change could more aptly be named the 'Wait and See' phase, for I was rather hesitant about what to do next. I was already following the children's interests for the implementation of themes, acting as a facilitator in their learning, and providing some guidance within the structure of the day by maintaining a somewhat flexible time-table. This form consisted of indoor activities with specialist sessions on some mornings, story group, snack time, book sharing period, outdoor activities, group time and the dismissal of morning group children. For the full day children this routine was followed by lunch, relaxation exercises and a short rest. After this period, games, specialist activities or outdoor experiences were introduced, then mat time and home time dismissal. Apart from these explanations I simply let it happen as the children's interest developed.

The following dialogue demonstrates how quickly the children utilised their newly designed room in order to create something of their own. Only a week after the writing area had been set up, Robbie walked in with a note book and pen. He greeted me with, 'Hi Bronwyn. I'm going to work in the office today'. He walked over to the writing area, sat down and proceeded to write in the note pad. Another child, Amelia, who heard this remark said, 'Bronwyn, we need a new sign that says, office'. This resulted in our writing area being turned into 'Our ELC Office'.

Some twenty minutes later Ned walked over to me and remarked, 'Bronwyn I've made you a newspaper for the office'. A friend overheard this comment and replied, 'Does it talk about the rain coming today'. The child replied, 'Yes! The meteorologist says it's going to be floods in Melbourne'. Their final comment suggested that they had better make sure our weather board said the same thing.

A few days later this same child was instrumental in making a pretend computer for the ELC Office, while his friend made the mouse and a mat. During the construction process Toby joined them and asked what they were doing. After being informed about their work, he suggested that they might like a printer, because it did the 'paper work'. His offer received a warm reception, so he

This drawing of 'Mrs Snoopy' was given to me by a 4 year old child. I was wearing a 'Snoopy' T shirt that day and the child only asked me to spell out the words 'Mrs' and 'Snoopy'.

set to work. After everything was completed the three children proudly placed their hand-crafted computer equipment in the ELC Office and quickly engaged in some 'pretend' office work. Ned used the computer keyboard to spell out his name, Amelia did some writing and Toby said he had to read the magazine to get some important information. They were engaging themselves in what they considered to be special office work.

What was important even at this early stage was the amount of control and appropriate direction the children were able to take with my guiding support. Observations also confirmed how the children were basing their literate acts in the context of meaningful experiences. What was different at this stage though was my higher focus on literacy. I could even see myself becoming

more confident in terms of developing the children's emergent literacy. In other words, I was now actively seeking to lead the children's literacy growth forward, while simultaneously applauding each of their literacy milestones. I describe these processes now.

A 4 year old child copying her friend's name from the name cards. Notice how several letters (a, r and e) have been transposed into capital letters

Establishing a love of books

It seemed appropriate to allocate a specific time in the morning when the children could select books to look at and read. The perfect time appeared to be directly after the children finished eating their snack. One by one as the children completed their washing up tasks, they would find a special spot either in the library area to look at books or story tapes, or on the story mat

The ELC Office – fully equipped with a pretend computer on the table

where big book sharing became popular, or they would interact with a story on the computer. Because I set aside times and places for using literature, the children came to know how I honoured books (Morrow, 1982). This segment became an accepted part of the day and if I ever forgot this routine, some child could be heard saying, 'But we haven't had book-sharing time yet!' Not only did they become enthusiastic about books but this procedure became a valued part of the pre-school program.

However, I found that it wasn't just reading to the children that made the difference, or providing excellent library facilities. It was enjoying the books with them and allowing them to become involved in the story (Heath, 1983). Before each story we talked

23

about the author, illustrator, and perhaps other books in the series. We often reflected on the books form and content, talked about the text, examined the print, discussed the meanings of words and talked about different writing conventions. The

A child's painting 'The Gingerbread Man', including h. name

children were fascinated with these aspects of books. One parent said to me that she couldn't understand why her daughter was going around the house shouting and then making a vertical line gesture with her hand, followed by a dot. When approached the child said, 'It's alright Mother, I'm just making an exclamation mark. We learnt about them in 'The Three Billy Goats Gruff' at pre-school today'.

Story time was a real favourite with the children and I'm sure that it was because the associated activities created such an

Book sharing time

Notice the exclamation marks!

interactive process for them. It meant employing different story-telling techniques and letting go as the teacher. We usually concentrated on the story for about a week and after this period the children often asked for it to be placed in the library corner with the little felt board. One may be asking, 'Why continue with the same story for so long?' Well, it was always the children's decision to do so and an educator can generally tell when it is time for a change. Not only did the children help to read the story, but one or two were chosen to assist the adult reader by placing the appropriate felt pieces on the board, whilst another child held up the cards. Appropriate flash cards were often used for punch-lines and this became an enjoyable inter-active process for the children.

It was remarkable how quickly the children came to recognise the words. When reading stories like 'The Gingerbread Man', I would wave my hand as the cue for the children to join in with, 'Run, run, as fast as you can. You can't catch me, I'm the gingerbread man'. The children became fascinated with these punch-line cards and if I didn't include them with the main story they would say, 'Bronwyn! Where are the writing cards to go with the story?' These cards also proved valuable in helping the children become familiar with writing conventions. It wasn't unusual for a child to call out excitedly during story time something like, 'Bronwyn! There's a full stop. Look! There's another one'. As Goodman (1986) notes, children come to know what to expect with written language. They start to predict how stories

This child was very excited because he had made a 'little' and a 'big' full stop

Two 3 year old children telling a story from memory to a small group of children

will start and what kind of language to expect. My observations suggest that they also become alert to punctuation marks.

The stories were carefully selected on the basis of theme relevance, repetitiveness, cumulativeness, rhyme, familiarity and enjoyment, so it was much easier for the children to become *au fait* with the story. Often, specially made puppets were used with the story and the children delighted in being puppeteers, or they dramatised the story using their own hand-made props. In some cases the children made up their own version of the story and, with the assistance of staff, copied the writing onto a word-processor. With so much activity for the one story, is it any wonder that they didn't tire of it quickly? It wasn't unusual to see children actually performing one of the stories from memory to

a small group, sitting with their legs crossed, pretending to read just like the teacher.

A child presenting the weather forecast on channel 9

The importance of routine

Another regular segment in the timetable was the weather forecast and this typically followed our story, so the children would inform me. The routine of particular formalities was becoming very important to the children. One day when Pippa was asked to be the meteorologist, Eliza suggested that she pretend to turn the TV on because that was where they gave weather forecasts. Alice said, 'Let's have channel 2 and count to two numbers'. Brent continued with ,'Yeah! But we really need a sign for 'on' and 'off', Bronwyn, and writing at the top that

An 'ad' break between reporting the News

says it's a TV'. Jodie added, 'We can pretend to be the audience, so remember mat time is listening time'.

Some time after a TV frame was drawn around the weather board, a child remarked, 'This is really silly 'cause on TV they say the news first'. I suggested that some children might like to make a TV out of a large cardboard box. I asked Ritchie if he could find out what writing was on his TV at home and he did so. The next day after the paint on the TV set was dry, Ritchie and Toby helped to copy the writing onto the word processor. Words like Rank Arena, On, Off and Power were then pasted onto the TV. A pretend news stand was found and each child took turns at presenting the news in brief and the weather forecast. One particular morning a child raced in and with a quick good morning greeting, headed directly towards the writing table, announcing 'I'm finding my name for the TV thing, 'cause I've got some news today'.

Inspirational developments

The following dialogue illustrates how this news broadcast activity developed further. One day, Ritchie was presenting the news in brief. He said, 'National Nine News by Brian Nail. An earthquake made a big explosion. Many buildings fall down. Now it's time for an ad break'. He raced over to our Travel Agency, picked up a brochure about the Gold Coast and declaimed, 'Holidaying in Queensland is great'. After this episode the children routinely took to interrupting their news in brief to present advertisements.

Similarly, a routine procedure developed with the letter-box opening. At this stage the children were writing lots of letters to the assistant teacher, their friends and to me. Because of the large quantity of mail, I suggested that we have a special postal delivery each day. The children decided that just before lunch would be a good time. I thought so too, since it meant that all children were included in this particular literacy activity, whichever time of day they attended.

If I ever forgot this letter-opening procedure at precisely the time agreed upon the children were once again quick to remind me. This session with the children was always great fun. I would pretend to be the very old-fashioned postman and would blow a whistle. The child chosen to empty the letter-box was helped, if they needed it, to read out the names on the envelopes. Admittedly, this became a way for the children to learn to recognise their friends' names quickly and it was all part of the game. The involvement of the children was so intense that the letter-opening ceremony soon developed much formality. One child suggested that we needed to get one of 'those letter knives',

Postal delivery time

so that we could open the letters up nicely. He said that he knew about them because his dad had one at the office. The next day I brought in a brass letter opener for the children and it became a regular prop for the event.

Transferring literacy

The following dialogue also verifies how the children were now transferring literacy acts into other areas of the integrated curriculum. During one mat time experience when we were discussing some guidelines, a hand went up and its owner said, 'Bronwyn! Why don't you write them down?' This idea was warmly accepted and the children continued their discussion about making rules. Another child suggested that I put them on cards just like the colours, shapes and numbers, because then they could be read at mat time, especially if children needed to

A letter posted to me in the ELC letter-box by a 4 year old child

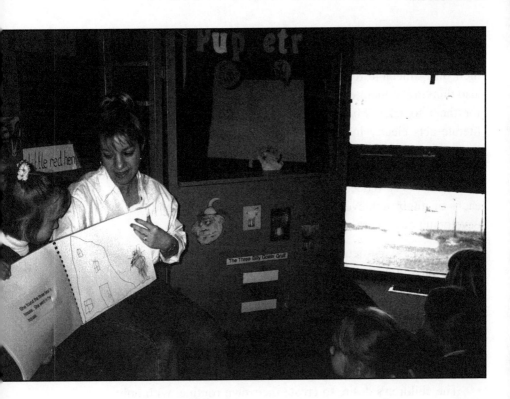

Story time

be reminded about appropriate behaviour. I followed this request through and also included illustrations to prompt the children with the message on each card. These became our 'ELC' rules.

The rule cards were used often by the children and as a teacher resource. On many occasions the children could be seen modelling me with the cards. A child would sit on my chair with legs crossed and the rule cards in hand, while several children sat on the mat and memorised the writing on the rule cards. They could be heard saying, 'Remember mat time is listening time. Remember to walk inside. Remember to behave sensibly and appropriately', and so on. It was wonderful to see.

33

Celebrating literacy

It was quite obvious to me that the children were developing their own timetable for their special literacy events. They were also thinking in literate ways because it was a 'natural' direction for them to take. My infinite observations of the children's literate acts clearly indicate the multiple pathways to literacy. Even though children follow similar patterns of development, each literacy milestone is unique to the individual (Roskos and Newman, 1994). Indeed, the children could see that I celebrated each of their achievements, unique expressions and their developing awareness of literacy, its functions and uses.

To recapitulate particular aspects pertinent to the children's literacy directions and sum up, then, the following developments needed to, and/or did, transpire:

• The restructuring of the classroom into a print-filled environment

• Making literacy provisions, including a permanent and centralised writing area for the children

• The children's desire to create their own routine, with only minor deviations when necessary

• Requests from the children to provide a certain amount of repetitiveness within the program, especially the rereading of stories; and

• My role as a facilitator in the children's learning of literacy.

PART 3
RUNNING ON WITHOUT ME

It soon became clear that my role as an early childhood educator was not to prepare children for literacy but to accept and extend what children already know about reading and writing. What I had become was a provider, facilitator and nurturer of the children's emerging literacy. Far from seeing the early literacy efforts of young children as just 'play', I concur with many other researchers and recognise these literate acts as significant developmental activities in the evolution of literacy (Ferreiro and Teberosky, 1983; Bruner, 1984; Harste, Woodward and Burke, 1984; Goodman, 1986).

Moreover, it became strongly evident that learning is futile if it lacks meaning for the children. Most importantly I realise how vital it is for teachers to communicate with children in order to 'scaffold' their learning. In doing so we assist children in their endeavours to make sense of the world. What I have discovered is that children need educators to explain things to them as well as tell them things. Like children, teachers, too, need to travel along a multitude of pathways in the pursuit of learning. 'As well as facilitating, teachers need to teach. The erroneous idea that children are never told or taught what to do may stem from research in classrooms where teachers were unsure of what was required of them' (Raban Bisby, 1995). And this is just how I used to feel.

With this renewed but continually developing philosophy I was not surprised that the children regarded and accepted literacy as a way of life within the classroom. Not only was I providing a literate environment for the children but I was drawing their attention to literacy. What evolved from this approach was a natural extension and incorporation of literacy acts into the weave of their curricular experiences (Newman and Roskos, 1990). In other words the number of literacy play themes grew, and during the web of events more and more children became involved in these literacy demonstrations. It was like a chain reaction. As Frank Smith would say, 'They join the literacy club' (1984), and that is what they did.

The children's hand-written class list

It all makes sense
Learning through meaningful contexts: indoors

Play and print were negotiated and interwoven into many areas of the children's play. During play experiences the use of paper and pencils was frequently evident. Children were often seen walking around the room with a clipboard, paper and pencil, engaging in 'pretend' writing or writing down their friends' names.

On one occasion when I asked a girl what she was doing she replied, 'Well, I've got a class list and I'm finding out who's here today because we're going on an excursion. You do that don't you Bronwyn? You tick the names off'. And, indeed, before we left for an excursion I always went through the protocol of calling out the children's names from a class list and if they were present I placed a tick next to their name. My question had been answered beautifully.

The following description and short narrative also stresses the importance of learning through meaningful contexts. The children's area of interest at this particular time was travel. One of their friends in the group was on a travelling vacation overseas and had sent the children numerous postcards. They decided that a four-wheel drive vehicle needed to be built so they could tour around Australia. A table turned upside down was used for the frame and cardboard poles held up the roof. The children retrieved an old steering wheel from the outdoor shed and placed a few chairs inside this vehicle for seating.

One day, several children decided they were going on a trip to the Northern Territory, but before they went they had to collect the passengers. I think the jeep had been turned into a bus. I thought it might be interesting to join them on their journey. Street and traffic signs had already been placed around the room, so I decided to wait at the sign labelled 'Bus Stop'.

A couple of children soon joined me at the stop. They asked me whether the writing on the pole said 'Bus Stop'. I told them it did and they sat down. When the bus driver called out, 'Hop on!' I proceeded. However, I was promptly greeted with, 'Sorry Bronwyn! You can't come because you haven't got a school uniform on and this is a school trip. Oh, it doesn't matter, we can just pretend you've got one on'. I hopped on and sat down in the back seat so I could see what was going on. I had a laugh to myself when the bus driver opened up a brochure on the Northern Territory and said, 'I'll have to find the road map that tells us how to get to Uluru, and then we'll be on our way'.

The pretend bus that took the school children to Uluru

It was also common to see children writing notes to one another, often indecipherable messages. They included signs, invitations, thank you notes, and letters to the staff, many of which were included into their play themes. Some of this correspondence was even posted in the letter box and routinely opened at mat time.

In fact the children were even embellishinging their drawings, paintings and art and craft work with writing or 'pretend' writing. They were writing on magna doodles, whiteboards, blackboards, the computer and forming words with magnetic letters.

> tobronwyn
>   abigai   loves   you   are alovely teacher . I have lots of friends, alix,
> clare, ellie, and jessica k.
> i had a nice day.
> from abi.

A letter written to me on the computer by one of the children
Below: A child rejoicing in his achievement at arranging the
magnetic letters into alphabetical order

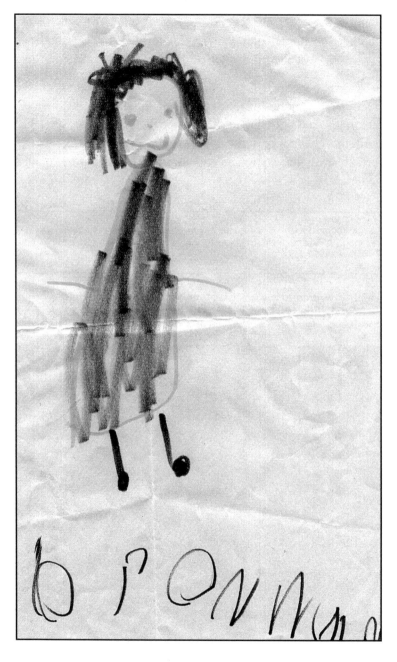

Examples of the children's writing, including names (left), labelling (right) and a letter to a friend (below right)

Lydia

CAMPU
LL
LI LYDIA

JESSICA
ATEBR

REDING
70% RECYCLED PAPER

They wrote labels and their names on their work, and if they couldn't write something they came and asked for the words to be written down so they could copy them. They were beginning to see how powerful writing could be, especially in the sense of ownership and recognition.

Outdoors

Predictably outdoor play is not quite as conducive to literacy acts as indoors. However, this did not stop the children. They were regularly found participating in literacy acts outside. Writing number-plates for their vehicles, writing down fire-call messages and writing out tickets for speeding motorists. It was also common to see children dictating pretend recipes to their friends while making apple pies outside, or for children to pretend to follow the recipe from a cookery book to make something for a picnic lunch.

The accessibility of the writing area to outdoor play was a great advantage. With the sliding double doors to the classroom open, the children could access it directly from the outside. They could be seen constantly going inside to make signs for their vehicles, to name their cubby house, to write down messages. Often they would collect some paper and a pen and take it outside to do their writing. An example of this follows: Adrian had just completed making a fire engine using wooden blocks, with the frame of a table being used to balance the steering wheel. He collected his props, which included a fire hat, rubber hose and a small wooden ladder. After sitting in the truck, he said to me, 'How will the

The 'Fire Truck' sign, written by a 4 year old child

children know if this is a fire engine?' I assured him that his construction, along with the accessories, gave the children plenty of clues. Obviously still not convinced, he raced inside and returned with paper and pen. 'How do you write fire truck, Bronwyn?' I wrote it down and he copied it. Then he went back inside and came out with some sticky tape and stuck it on the front of the vehicle.

Social matters

The creation of signs and lists to help solve conflicts that occurred during play was often done during mat time. It was common to observe a group of children and an adult discussing writing and posting rules for tidy-up time, as part of a social problem-solving interaction. Literacy was used to assist the social concerns of the group. The children often seized staff members' offers to serve as scribes on these matters. These literacy events were used to serve the peer dynamics of their core group in several ways: they permitted them to articulate their interests and also helped them to protect and define their space from the intrusion of others. The power of print was also used by several children to reaffirm their leadership, for example, 'I'm the boss!' says one girl to another. 'I'm doing the writing so you can be the little baby'. Notes were also written to reaffirm friendships like, 'I love you'.

A note to me with the child's telephone number on it, just in case I wanted to contact her during the holidays

A 'love' note from one of the children

Because he was concerned about the block building a child asked me to write a sign that read, 'Please do not knock over the building'. He copied the writing and then stuck it to the construction

Becoming authors and illustrators

As well as becoming 'readers and writers', some children wanted to know if they could become authors and illustrators. I believe this particular interest stemmed from my focus on books. I have discribed how, before starting our mat time story, we always read the title of the book and the author's name. However, this protocol was extended at the children's request. They wanted to know if I could write the author's name on a card as well, just like I had with the title, and stick it to the felt board and so it happened. An example being, 'Today our story is 'The Bus Stop' by Nancy Hellen'.

We then talked about the illustrator. The children enjoyed doing this, especially the child selected to assist with the felt pieces to accompany the story, because they liked to point to the words as the children read them. You could see how proud this assisting child felt, for the children saw this activity as an honourable and very special role.

A child copying words from a book onto the computer

The felt story-board

On one occasion during group experience there was a suggestion from a child that we write our own version of 'The Three Billy Goats Gruff'. Naturally I was delighted at this proposal, so children on the mat took turns at being an author. It was made more interesting when, as I started to write down their lines, a voice called out, 'Why don't you write it on the big paper and put it on the easel? That way we could all see it'. What a brilliant idea! Before continuing with the story, we gathered this equipment together and the children continued dictating their version of the story. As the story was a long one, we also decided that it would be a good idea to work on this task a bit each day. It became their project and their work. After the story was completed they asked if they could copy the writing onto the computer and this they did. Concurrently, other children were being illustrators and drawing the pictures.

Before compiling the book we listed the names of all the young authors and illustrators. The children watched the binding process and this book became their pride and joy. They were so excited that some of the children even took it home on different occasions to show and read to their parents.

Becoming literate thinkers:
from pre-school to home or is it home to pre-school?

In general, I believe these countless informal writing experiences formed a pathway for the children towards understanding the power and functions of print and to reading itself. Indeed, Clay (1991) contends that 'the first explorations of print in the pre-school years may occur in writing rather than reading' (p.108).

The children were undoubtedly becoming literate thinkers. Many parents reported that their children wanted to write letters or invitations to post in the letter box we had in our room, or make bookmarks for their friends.

This child copied the writing 'The Three Little Pigs', from the cover of a book

Writing on lunch order bags also became popular and several preschoolers even had their siblings helping them with certain writing procedures. Several parents told me that they could no longer even read a story without talking about the author, illustrator and whether there were other books in the series. One child even reported to her father that they had different 'virgins' of Goldilocks. He was so puzzled that he conferred with his wife, who told him how they had been talking about different versions of 'Goldilocks and The Three Bears'.

Another parent told us that her son asked if he could have some of his father's old ties and that when she asked why he said that he wanted to put on a puppet play for his family. The ties, he explained, were so he could hang up an old sheet and hide behind it. Apparently this child delighted the family, including his grandparents, with a performance of 'The Little Red Hen'. After telling me about this incident, the mother asked whether, as they had videotaped this performance, her son could bring it in to show his friends. The children were so impressed with the tape that they wanted to watch it again. Although this wasn't feasible, it did inspire us to film some of our own puppet shows.

The sharing of children's literacy acts at home had never happened with such intensity before. I'm sure one contributing factor was my involving parents in the development of their children's literacy celebrations. Once again it set off a chain effect. Parents saw me supporting their children's literacy learning, so they wanted to share their children's literacy acts and achievements with me. Clearly, fundamental to all forms of parental involvement is a two way communication path between home and school and I knew what might open up these 'gates' even more. A natural extension then to this literacy program was to develop and organise several information nights for the parents, entitled 'Literacy Before Schooling – Parents as Partners'.

A bookmark one of the children made for her friend, Annette

The story of 'Goldilocks and the Three Bears' written and illustrated by the children.

48

PART 4
PARENTS AS PARTNERS

I know now that there is considerable potential for involving parents in the pre-school teaching of literacy. Indeed, we have a great deal to learn about it from parents. After all, they spend many hours with their pre-school children engaging in literacy acts (Hannon and James, 1990). Are they not, therefore, as experienced in this area as we early childhood educators are? Why is it then that many of us discourage parents from focusing on their children's literacy learning? Is it because we feel they may teach children the wrong way, or that it may place too much pressure on them? How many pre-school teachers really know how primary school teachers approach literacy and what do we mean by too much pressure? Perhaps the answer to these questions lies in the fact that we don't have the skills anyway. Could it be that this lack of knowledge about early literacy is what creates a lack of confidence in our ability to tackle children's literacy in the program? If this isn't the case, then why are we not articulating our approach to reading and writing in the pre-school curriculum to the parents?

The front cover of a child's book, 'The Little Red Hen'

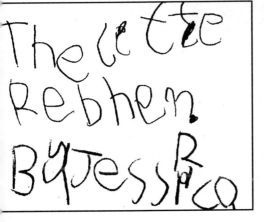

Children sharing story time with their dads at a special pre-school night

These comments are certainly not intended as derogatory towards the competence of pre-school teachers. The reason for sharing such statements and posing such questions is because this is the way I felt before I started to reflect on this area of the pre-school curriculum. Even though I was inwardly questioning my philosophy and pedagogy, outwardly it was easier for me to approach this subject area from a pre-reading and pre-writing perspective, because I didn't know what else to do.

To address this apathy and grow as an educator, I needed to embrace processes of self-evaluation and self-analysis in relation to my classroom and early childhood practices. And now here I am, a more relaxed, confident and wiser teacher, with an emergent literacy perspective. My understanding now is that literacy means accepting and extending what children already know about reading and writing. Naturally, this means building onto the tradition of a child-centred approach and making provisions for literacy. It means working with parents and sharing knowledge with them about how children learn; it means listening to their concerns relating to their children's literacy learning; and it means celebrating the children's achievements with them.

Parents' role in their children's literacy

If we accept the notion that a great deal of children's literacy learning takes place in the home, how can we as educators justify excluding parents from this area of their children's education? Parents play vital roles in providing the foundation for emerging literacy. A parent is not only a child's first tutor but their one enduring source of faith that somehow, sooner or later, they will become a reader and writer (Education Department of Western Australia, 1995).

Coming from an emergent literacy perspective, where attention is focused on the naturally acquired beginning of literacy and therefore on the home and the parents (Hannon,1990), led me to my next adventure: organising a series of information nights for the parents on 'Literacy Before Schooling'. The foundations for these sessions were based on the recognition that early childhood programs build on the successful learning provided in the home by parents. A key first step was to highlight the importance of parents and teachers working together in partnership to promote the children's learning.

Furthermore, I stressed to the parents that often the best educators are enthusiastic educators. For if we are enthusiastic about teaching and learning, particularly literacy, our children will be empowered to love learning and become passionate about literacy.

An example of some of the literacy provisions talked about at the writing session with parents

The other point to convey to the parents was that in most cases parents were already doing the 'right thing' towards developing their children's literacy. So I simply wanted to affirm our partnership. The literacy sessions were therefore to reassure parents and give them confidence to carry on their work.

The sessions were basically divided into reading and writing. Another concentrated on story time and the importance of

DEAR LYDIA

ENJOY YOUR LUNCH TODAY. IF YOU EAT IT ALL THERE IS A SPECIAL SURPRISE FOR YOU.

LOVE BRUCE.

P.S. HAVE A GOOD DAY.

P.S.S. MUMMY AND HAYDEN SEND ALL OUR LOVE ALWAYS. xxxx.

Dearest Jorja

Remember to tell Bronwyn that Nana Murphy is picking you up today.

Have fun!

Lots of Love Mummy xx oo

°ANNE GEDDES

Several letters discovered in the children's lunch boxes, from their parents

5 JESSICA

LOVE You !

HAVE A NICE DAY.

LOVE MUMMY

enjoying books with young children. The only reason for splitting up reading and writing as aspects of literacy was to help parents think about them one at a time – but I emphasised that the two are woven together and how one continually influences the other.

The sessions on 'Reading and the Home' and 'Writing and the Home', included a short talk on how young children learn and how their parents could work with me as partner in the development of their children's literacy. I suggested how they might provide a rich reading and writing environment for the children giving concrete examples about how they could help, and showing them a variety of literacy provisions which enhance this area of the children's development. I reminded the parents that they probably had these resources anyway and that the vital ingredient here was our approach towards literacy. A memorandum handout on different strategies was provided for the parents to refer to. The evenings concluded with an information sharing period and discussion time.

SESSION 1
Reading and the home

The general reaction from parents to the literacy sessions was overall appreciation. Of the eighteen parents present during the first session relating to reading, seventeen mentioned how they enjoyed it because it gave them strategies for approaching reading, and support for their role in their children's reading. It seemed that these parents already provided books, equipment and time to assist their children becoming literate but were unsure about how to help them develop further. Three parents thought that they could be 'doing it all wrong', and two expressed concern about not wanting to push their children. After the session, however, the general consensus was that they felt more confident, especially in their ability to assist their young child's reading development in a 'natural way'.

One parent was absolutely delighted when her son brought home a book that the children had written and illustrated as a group. She said:

> When my son showed my husband and me the version of 'The Three Billy Goats Gruff' book that they made, we were really excited. He read out all the names of the authors and illustrators without any hesitation, and was especially excited when he came to his name. Then he pretended to read the story. Actually I think he memorised it almost word for word. We were really impressed with this and told him so.

Another said:

> Can you believe at the weekend my husband and I spent two hours with the children going through the cupboard looking for books starting with 'once upon a time'. They told us that they were talking about books that begin like this, and they wanted to find some so they could share them with their friends at book sharing time.

The Library Area

SESSION 2
The Story Time session

The story time session focused mainly on the importance of enjoying books with the children. My comments in chapter one about books formed the foundations for this session. Once again I gave the parents a handout, only this time it included a list of recommended books for sharing with pre-school children. Advice to the parents to read to their children would appear to be sound, and likely to promote the development of literacy. But in this case it would have been unnecessary – the parents needed no prompting to read to their children. Instead, they needed advice on how to help their children when they showed an interest in reading. Eleven out of the fifteen parents also indicated that they never even thought about focusing on such aspects as the print, where the story starts, occasionally pointing to the words as you read, the directionality of reading and so forth. The following comments confirm this area of the parents' need.

> *I gained a lot from the strategies you gave us. Even though I read to my child constantly I never really thought of talking much about the authors, illustrators, the rhyming words – you know, that type of thing.*

> *The session on picture story books was great. I'll try not to hurry the reading any more, for now I realise that there isn't much point in doing it that way. I liked the way you talked about sometimes pointing to the words as you read and also about where to start. Those sorts of aspects.*

As a special focus to this session, I invited a story-teller as a guest speaker. He was a great entertainer also, and his enthusiasm alone was an inspiration to all of us to read books with such passion. The majority of parents said they enjoyed this session, because it gave them some insights into what to look for when buying books for their children.

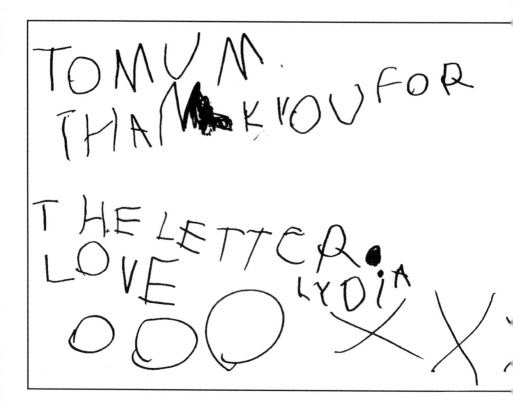

A child's thank you letter to her mum

SESSION 3
Writing and the home

The 'Writing and the home' session received a response from the parents similar to that on reading. Thirteen parents attended and again the overall reaction was that they found the strategies for helping their children's writing development very helpful. The parents in attendance all confirmed that they provided writing materials for their children but ten of them observed that they hadn't thought of providing such a variety of equipment.

Four parents, however, did mention their anxiety over whether they should teach their children to write in capital or 'little' letters, and two parents said they were unsure about whether to say the alphabet using, 'Ay', 'Bee', 'See', or 'ah','buh', 'kuh'.

The following comments and narratives will, I hope, help to encapsulate some of the parents' thoughts, concerns and aspirations relating to their children's literacy development and to the sessions.

I found the lectures on 'Literacy before Schooling' both interesting and informative. It is both encouraging and refreshing to find such an enthusiastic and passionate teacher in the early learning sector. A teacher that believes in the children's ability to grasp the concepts of reading and writing. So many teachers pigeon-hole our children and believe that they are only capable of learning to read and write at certain ages.

By attending the lectures parents have been given a sound understanding and guidelines to teach literacy in the home. As parents we can provide continuity with the same teaching methods that are provided at pre-school.

And:

> *Thank you for finding the time to present to the parents your wonderful 'Parents as Partners' literacy program. Not only was the information extremely relevant and useful but it also made me realise that I can, with confidence, help my child without feeling that I am going about it all wrong, or that I will spoil what will be done in prep the following year.*
>
> *Your ideas are easy to implement and very practical. I also now realise that it is because of your provision of such an enriching environment for the children in your program and your incredible flexibility in allowing the children to run with their ideas and to experiment with reading and writing.*

A few days after the series of information sessions had finished I received several letters of appreciation. One parent wrote:

> *I only wish my other daughter had the same opportunity. This year I feel as if I have been a real partner in my child's learning, especially in the area of literacy.*

Summary

There is no doubt that the parents at my school were interested in their children's emerging literacy. So if pre-school teachers wish to extend children in every area of their development, there seems no reason to exclude the area of literacy. Parents who have children asking about words and letters on a daily basis would surely lose confidence in the teacher who told them: 'Actually literacy development isn't a part of the program; we only concentrate on pre-reading and pre-writing skills. Anyway the children learn through play'. My response would be to ask: why not integrate aspects of literacy into the children's socio-dramatic and exploratory play? If we really believe in the importance of home/school communication as educators, we need to listen to parents as well as talk to them. Besides, the general consensus is that parents are their children's first and most influential teacher.

What transpired from this enrichment program is a desire to illustrate to other early childhood educators and parents of preschool age children the ways in which children learn to read and write. We need to change our traditional views on how children learn literacy and alter our methods accordingly. Holdaway (1980) aptly describes this new direction when he says that literacy is learned by children rather than taught by teachers. We are the children's guiding support.

References

Bruner, J (1984) Language, Mind and Reading. In H. Goelman, J. Oberg, and F. Smith (Eds.), *Awakening to Literacy* (pp, 193-200). London: Heinemann.

Clay, M. (1991) *Becoming Literate*. London: Heinemann.

David, T. (1990) *Under Five – Under-Educated?* Buckingham: Open University Press.

Education Department of Western Australia. (1995) *Parents as Partners*. Melbourne: Longman Australia

Ferreiro, E., and Teberosky, A. (1983) *Literacy Before Schooling*. London: Heinemann.

Goodman, K. (1982) *Language and Literacy*. Volume 1. *Process, Theory, Research*. London: Routledge and Kegan Paul.

Goodman, Y. (1986) Children coming to know literacy. In W. Teale and E. Sulzby (Eds.), *Emergent Literacy* (pp.1-14). Norwood, NJ: Ablex.

Hall, N. (1987) *The Emergence of Literacy*. London: Hodder and Stoughton.

Hannon, P. (1990) Parental Involvement in Preschool Literacy Development. In Wray, D. (Ed.), *Emerging Partnerships*: Current Research in Language and Literacy. BERA Dialogues in Education, No4. Clevedon: Multilingual Matters.

Hannon, P. and James, S. (1990) Parents' and Teachers' Perspectives on Pre-school Literacy Development. *British Educational Research Journal* 16, 259-272.

Harste, J., Woodward, V., and Burke, C. (1984) *Language Stories and Literacy Lessons*. London: Heinemann.

Heath, S. B. (1983) *Ways with Words*: Language, Life and Work in Communities and Classrooms. Cambridge. Cambridge University Press.

Holdaway, D. (1980) *Independence in Reading*. Gosford: Ashton Scholastic.

Kantor, R., Miller, S., and Fernie, S. (1992) Diverse Paths to Literacy in a Preschool Classroom: A Sociocultural Perspective. *Reading Research Quarterly*. 27, 185-201.

Morrow, L. (1982) Relationships between Literature Programs, Library Corner Designs, and Children's Use of Literature. *Journal of Educational Research*, 75, 339-344.

Newman, S., and Roskos, K. (1990) Play, Print, and Purpose: Enriching Play Environments for Literacy Development. *The Reading Teacher*, 44, 214-221.

Raban-Bisby, B. (1995) What do we know about how young children learn? *Victorian School News*. Melbourne: Ministry of School Education.

Roskos, K. and Newman, S. (1994) Of Scribbles, Schemas and Storybooks: Using Literacy Albums to Document Young Children's Literacy Growth. *Young Children*, January, 78-85.

Smith, F. (1984) *Joining The Literacy Club*. Victoria B.C. Centre for the Teaching of Reading and Abel Press.

Vygotsky, L.S. (1962) *Thought and Language*. Cambridge: M.I.T. Press.

GK00707352

The Amazing Dan

by
Barry L. Hillma..

"The Amazing Dancing Bear" was an Award Winner in the Bristol Old Vic. Harris Best Play Competition in 1981. It went on to have it's premiere with the Questors Theatre, Ealing in 1981, and it's professional premiere was at The Leeds Playhouse in 1985 directed by John Harrison.

Characters

Evie	*a child of 10*
Barney	*bear owner*
Otto	*the bear*
Sir Francis	*landowner*
Lady Ellen	*his wife*
Isadore	*his daughter*
Horatio	*her suitor*
Raddles	
Con	*Evie's mother*
Arthur	*her husband*
Isiah	*workman*
Oliver	*workman*
Terry	*teenager*
Townfolk	

ACT I Scene 1

1814. Blackness. A piercing scream. It is a child's voice. A single dim spotlight illuminates little EVIE. She is a rickets thin girl of 10, but her diminutive frame and spindle shanks give her the appearance of a 7 or 8 year old. Her shrunken consumptive face is filled with fear and if she had energy to cry, she would. She is alone in a vast expanse of night. - A small clearing in a wood on the outskirts of the town of Stone Marston in the fast industrialising Midlands.

EVIE: I en't frit of you! 'On't do no good skulking rained trees - *(A black shape brushes past her, almost overbalancing her. She cries out in alarm.)* Ahh! I en't done nothin' t'you, why should you want to scare a body? Jesus'll ;eve yer! Argh - *(Once again the form collides with her and this time sends her spinning to the ground. Blackberries tipple out of the pinafore she has been doubling up in front of her.)* Mercy, dun't kill me! You've squashed me blackberries. Mum, mum!

BARNEY: *(appearing with a lantern).* God 'elp us, what's gewing on? Anybody'ld think you wus bein' murdered. *(They both speak with a Northamptonshire accent.)*

EVIE: *(in fright).* Dun' 'it me - dun' 'it me!

BARNEY: "Dun' 'it me"? Why, what kind of a tain it is that ivery child thinks an adult's gewing t' 'it it? 'Ere, give me yer 'and, gel. You didn't oughta be ate in the woods at this time of night.

EVIE: *(pathetically trying to gather up the bruised blackberries).* I were being chased.

BARNEY: Chased? Niver in yer life!

EVIE: I were black berrying and got off the path. *(Fearfully indicating with thumb.)* You in with 'im?

BARNEY: 'Im?

EVIE: Big feller, lurching through the brambles. You gonna rape me?

BARNEY: Lord, what's a kiddie like you know of rape? There's nobody there but night creatures.

EVIE: *(as a form looms).* There! There!

BARNEY: *(laughing).* Why that's nowt but Otto! 'E's bin to relieve 'imself in the woods and is loster 'an what you are. *(Calls.)* Here, boy!

EVIE: *(in agitation).* Dun't bring 'im over 'ere.

BARNEY: You wouldn't separate a man from his brother?

EVIE: Brother? - I'm gunna 'ave a brother. Me mum's carrying 'im now. She was a' craving fruit. That's why I were black berrying.

BARNEY: Me ma were frit by a Russian when she were a'carrying me.

'Thought we'ld be twins, but I come ate 'uman and the other were Otto. Here lad - old feller!

EVIE: *(drawing back, but held by the hand by BARNEY)*. Aa -. *(As OTTO approaches into the light.)* It's the Devil, an 'airy devil!

BARNEY: It's a bear, y'ninny. Nothin' but a tame bear.

(BARNEY and the bear embrace. OTTO is over six feet and walks mostly on his hind legs. He is deep brown and immensely powerful but gentle. BARNEY is a ruddy, wrinkled man of 46, but looks nearer 60 with his wizened features and bent back.)

EVIE: *(disbelieving)*. I en't never seen a bear as big as that.

BARNEY: Well he's a Russian Dancing Bear, aren't you, Otto, old boy? Back on yer collar. *(He tethers the bear.)* Give 'im a pat.

EVIE: *(petulant)*. *I* en't touchin' 'im. 'E med me spill me blackberries!

BARNEY: Oh 'e'll say sorry fer that, won't you, Otto? *(OTTO squats on his haunches and puts his claws together two or three times in supplication.)* See? 'E's a spectacle of Repentance.

EVIE: *(titters)*. Silly!

BARNEY: You should see 'im juggle.

EVIE: Bears dun't juggle.

BARNEY: Russian ones does. *(He takes balls from his pocket and hands them to the bear who immediately juggles with them. EVIE is highly diverted.)*

EVIE: 'E's not your brother.

BARNEY: True as I stand 'ere. We were Christened in the sayme church and travelled in the sayme baby-carriage, only Otto got 'airier and 'airier and niver learned 'is alphabet.

EVIE: God dun't let people become bears.

BARNEY: Oh? And who're you that you're so well acquainted with the Almighty? *(EVIE is mute. OTTO sits and BARNEY sits beside him, clutching the girl's arm and pointing out into the sky.)* I tell you God's a yuge livin' wheel, spinning in the universe of space, and He spins s'fast bits of living matter fly off Him and lands on the planets, and evolves into fishes, then beasts, then men. And they wax and they suffer and cross their species and their genders and copulate and rot, but God dun't pay 'em no mind - no more 'an you would mind the filings off yer nails, even though they was part of yer own body. And Otto crossed his species, and danced, and God laughed.

EVIE: *(excited).* Let 'im dance f'me!

BARNEY: *(sly).* You 'en't God.

EVIE: God dun't care. I do!

BARNEY: You've 'it the nail on the 'ead, gel. God kent mayke a bear dance, only yuman will ken do that. *(He goes to a small tarpaulin-covered cart and extracts a ballet dress.)* On with the costume, Otto. Got a royal performance t'night. *(fixes tutu round bear's waist).* Dence, 'airy brither, dence! *(OTTO dances. BARNEY plays accordion or barrel-organ. Other townsfolk gather to see the sight, till they are in a lantern lit circle round the performers. Observing that he has attracted a crowd.)* And now, ladies and gentlemen, a series of acrobatics and tumbling feats by this amazing creature!

(Applause and "oohhs" and "aahs" as OTTO goes through his routine.) Next;- the first presentation in this area of the world's only uni-vellocopedic quadruped! (BARNEY produces a one wheeled cycle on which OTTO performs his act. Generous applause as BARNEY and EVIE tour the crowd collecting money in a hat. The performance ends with OTTO doing his "praying hands" trick.)*

SIR FRANCIS: *(stepping forward into the playing area).* And now, my friends, for your further edification a short spectacle entitled The Collective Wit and the Proletariate. *(Ordering.)* Men;- the Machines!

(a number of stitching machines are brought into the clearing. The crowd are silent. SIR FRANCIS choreographs himself around the machines.)

SIR FRANCIS: Now you all know me;- I am Sir Francis Sedley - the man upon whose private woods you are at present trespassing. I own the local factory which manufactures high-grade footwear, and for my services to industry I was Knighted. Yonder my wife *(With a gesture.)* Lady Ellen, my daughter, Isadore and her suitor Horatio. *(The three make acknowledgements.)* These are my latest machines for sewing and under- trimming leather, on the which a man can make as many pairs of shoes in a day as the old cottage cobbler could hand stitch in a month. A miracle of mechanical inventiveness, you might think, designed to make their operators productive and richer men. Not a bit of it. To the ignorant they are the tools of the Devil and of Capitalist Exploiters. Ignorance is the father of Fear; and Fear is the begetter of Violence. *(To the men in the crowd.)* Gentlemen - what ceremony of welcome have you devised for these Innovators of Progress - these overtures to end exploitation of the indigenous artisan?

(RADDLES, an agitator, and the town's workmen, band themselves into a noisy mob and hurl themselves at the machines, armed with a multitude of motley weapons - sickled, sledgehammers, pitchforks, and the like - with which they break the machines into heaps of scrap metal. Chaos. Screams. Battles between the wreckers and Sedley's supporters. BARNEY and OTTO cling to each other in terror. RADDLES and SIR FRANCIS face one another.)

SIR FRANCIS: You're a provider of employment, Raddles, I'll give you that. I provide work for the shoemen, and you create it for the mechanics!

RADDLES: You kent prove it were me as destroyed your machines.

SIR FRANCIS: No. No-one could be found to testify against you. Bully-boys fight oppression with oppression.

RADDLES: We've been indoctrinated by the capitalists into believing that the phoney notion that slaving for wages is somehow fine and natural - that doing something we hate, for money to spend on things we don't want - is some sort of freedom. Balls! It niver made the capitalists feel guilty about all the freedom and leisure they got out of our sweat. What we want is not freedom to work, but the freedom to work at what we *want* to work at. - The trouble with the working classes is that if you tek the old notion of toil away from them they've got nothing to put in it place.

SIR FRANCIS: And the trouble with equalitarians and agitators is that they think the difference between the working-classes and the nobility is money. Give the workers wealth and education and they'll develop the same vices as their masters! To be idealistic and incorruptible isn't the prerogative of the impoverished. I'm all for equality: even maintain that the rich should be treated with as much humanity as the poor. But facts, Raddles - I'm a man for facts: and the venality of Man is a fact.

RADDLES: It's also a fact that eight year old kids work in mines, with their lungs full of coal-dust and their phlegm black with it -yis, and womin too, hauling carts in tunnels three foot high: stripped to the waist: it's also a fact that the weavers work in twelve- hour shifts, and that cottage-workers have to compete with factory workers when trade is bad - to set brother against brother for the likes of you.

ISADORE: *(of RADDLES)* . You must admit there's something thrilling about the man's revolutionary oratory.

HORATIO: *(effete but shrewd)*. The sexual attraction of the activist for the pacifist, that is all.

EVIE: *(running to her parents)*. Mum! Mum! I made the bear dance.

CON: *(grabbing her)*. And I'll make *you* dence, y'little bugger, if you dun't tell me what you've dun with that money I gev yer.

EVIE: Money?

CON: F'yer dad's ale. *(To a neighbour.)* Kids en't nothing but empty 'eads and empty bellies. I've enuff of 'em nay, and if I could lose one I'm carrying presently I'ld be grateful.

NEIGHBOUR: The beast were a rare sight, though. I've not seen a turn like that.

BARNEY: *(proudly)*. Human-beings travel slowly behind Art.

ISIAH: *(poking OTTO with a stick)*. He'ld dence fer anyone who'd a musician's baton t'tickle his arse with! *(The bear attacks his tormentor. The crowd screams.)* Ah! The brute's crushing me bones! Git 'im orf! *(RADDLES struggles with the bear to release ISIAH.)*

ISADORE: *(admiringly)*. Oh the stout fellow! The native courage of the proletariat!

HORATIO: Tcha! He'ld be better to have the courage to leave a bully to its desserts.

BARNEY: *(entering the fracas)*. Leave, boy! Let him dane, Otto - leave! *(the bear obeys)*.

ISIAH: It's a wild thing. A menace. Oughta be pit dane afore it kills someone.

ELLEN: Nonsense. God's creatures are not to be bated.

BARNEY: It's a truth you're telling, m'lady. This very animal once led a fearful life as bait in a bear pit for ruffians to beat on. I rescued him myself, and no Daniel could 'ev 'ad a better nor a more grateful, lion.

SIR FRANCIS: And you aim to pasture this brute on my land - where there's expensive game to be harmed?

ISIAH: *(both ingratiating and insinuating).* You're right, sir. Wi' times sew uncertin and a man not knowing where 'is job'll gew next, 'e dun't need ne lessons from itinerants in theivin'. They incite men t'mayhem - y've seen it in this very tain. It'll be murder and anarchy next;

ISADORE: Oh, papa - let the man camp here. He'll do no harm, and my tutor has informed me that bears are vegetarians.

SIR FRANCIS: Well, if that's a fact, I'll respect it. But he's to light no fires, and if he strays into a trap he'll have only himself to blame. *(He begins to walk away. Laughing.)* Let him dance a' one leg, eh? That'll make him hop! Come along, Madam,*(To ELLEN.)* And, Warden, see these people off my property.

BARNEY: *(to ISADORE).* Thank you, Missy. There'll be a grand performance on the market square for all who care to witness it, and Otto will dance gratefully for his patroness, I'll be bained.

HORATIO: *(pleasantly to ISADORE as he takes her and leads her off).* Patronising cow.

(Exeunt aristocrats one way, villagers the other.)

EVIE: *(rushing to kiss the bear).* I shall see you agin then, Otto.

ISIAH: *(to her father as he takes her away).* See he dun't top your young'un, Arthur! Animals have hot ways..

CON: *(disgustedly throwing away the fruit).* Berries! The idle brat. That were yesterday's liking.

(Exeunt omnes, BARNEY and OTTO R, the others L.)

RADDLES: *(to his cronies as they depart).* There shall be fair poaching t'night, lads - and the bear kin tek the blame!*(Fade.)*

Scene 2

(Stacey Hall. The family dining, attended.)

ELLEN: Ought you to have given that performing gipsy permission to camp here, Sir Francis? I shan't feel safe in my bed this night.

SIR FRANCIS: *(sardonic).* I'm sure *you* could feel safe in your bed any night, my dear. It was a spontaneous gesture to stop the crowd siding with Raddles. As a Christian you should appreciate the generosity.

ELLEN: Generosity, like charity, begins at home. I would have to be a politician to appreciate the motives behind your generosities - not a Christian. Beliefs don't make one a fool.

SIR FRANCIS: On the contrary, my dear, they do just that. Belief in religious creeds has kept their factions merrily murdering each other for thousands of years: belief in political dogmas has done the same and gives agitators like Raddles a meaning to their sordid existence.

HORATIO: And on the national level it gives us Bonapartes.

SIR FRANCIS: Quite. Both religious and secular beliefs promise us wisdom and show us nothing but folly.

ISADORE: Yet, papa, Raddles may still be right, industrialisation can bring injustices.

SIR FRANCIS: As can all new methods. The labour forces have their unions and their friendly societies to care for them.

ISADORE: And their children?

SIR FRANCIS: Families used to work in units: if you're going to take them from their homes into factories, you've got to take the whole family or break it up.

ISADORE: Still -

SIR FRANCIS: 'Still' nothing. What this world needs is *less* belief, not more.

ELLEN: Oh you, you've no faith in anything. Faith has kept whole countries civilised through the centuries.

SIR FRANCIS: Practice helps us to commit our mistakes more perfectly.

HORATIO: *(languidly, but not to be out-done at dining-table axioms).* I always feel that life isn't so much "deja vu" as "Deja dit".

(They ignore him.)

ELLEN: I suppose you don't believe in money either.

SIR FRANCIS: I don't believe in it, but I like it. I can handle it and make it. That's a fact. Always facts, my dear.

ELLEN: *(soliloquy, unheard by the others).* He's an unsympathetic man: oh, a fair , rational one - a true descendant of the Age of Reason: but how can you argue with a man who has no opinions? How can you love a mind composed of facts? I don't love him, but I feel guilty that I've failed him. I've provided him with a factual wife, but I've not been caring enough. That's why I embrace religion: I thought it would bring warmth into my life: but I don't like people any better for it and that makes me feel bitter and lonely. Perhaps to love God is to love only the perfect - I mean, Isadore's a dutiful daughter; bright and open. I ought to think the world of her, but I just resent her - her youth, her looks, and her captivating sodomitical sailor.

SIR FRANCIS: When do you rejoin your ship, Horatio?

HORATIO: In a fortnight, sir. With Boney at rest on Elba the navy has no powerful need of me yet!

SIR FRANCIS: The service have been saying that Boney is finished for years. What is it this time? Naval strategy?

HORATIO: Good heavens, no. Economics, I should imagine.

ISADORE: Don't be too much of a hero, sir. I shall need a husband with all his limbs.

HORATIO: *(unheard aside).* Indeed, she speaks the truth there! *(Aloud.)* And I shall do my best to preserve those limbs the better to do service to your beauty, ma'am. *(Unheard.)* I shall fuck the first pretty recruit I see and quite forget her for the duration; But marriage is a social commitment one neglects at one's peril. Women and society require the status quo of it: men require the alibi of it. Besides, she's a passionate little thing. All her zeal and ardour for people and ideas is nothing more than sheer sexual energy, but she's not to know that yet. She'll have *something* in trousers if I don't cage it soon. I daresay we shall make a passable financial and amiable establishment.

SIR FRANCIS: Politicians make wars and businessmen win them, eh? I'm not sure that's not just truism, but it's been a good dinner, and it suits me to think it original. The boot-and-shoe industry will do its share. It'll be an easier revolution than Raddles would like, you'll see. We'll not make the mistakes the mines and mill-owners are making.

ISADORE: I suppose the assumption is that if people make greater quantities of goods they'll get paid more and the goods themselves will be cheaper, so they'll gain twice?

ELLEN: Yes, but won't goods have to be expendable before that works?

SIR FRANCIS: Well, what's more expendable than shoes?

ISADORE: *(arch).* People, perhaps?

ELLEN: Isadore, it isn't smart to be flippant about the Lord's children. You'll follow your father into free-thinking.

SIR FRANCIS: She could do worse. Strikes me a religion's father figure should look after his own, not let each species he creates eat each other.

ISADORE: God's may think they're powerful, but they can't put their arms round you. *(Giggles at HORATIO.)*

ELLEN: This is a irreligious house, Horatio. If my daughter consents to marrying you in a church I shall have achieved my only victory.

HORATIO: One must respect the ceremonies of the tribe, ma'am.

ISADORE: *(to audience).* It's very reassuring to the menfolk for us ladies to play the amusing silly-geese role from time to time that they've chosen for us. If it stops them feeling threatened, that's good sense: but father is indulgent, and Horatio is smug. They've both shocks awaiting them once I'm mistress of a household of my own. Father should have a son to inherit the little business empire he's so busy building. I've an inferiority complex about having failed him in my gender; yet never once in my entire life time has either parent reproached me for my failure to be a boy. I shall make it up to them, and myself, by developing a solid business head and becoming a force to be reckoned with in the management. Why shouldn't a factory wall bear the legend"Sedley and *Daughter*" as its sign, for a change? As for Horatio, he cynically assumes that sensuous playthings with nothing in their minds but men, will be blissfully content and domesticated if you push a regular sugar-plum in their mouths and something the same shape regularly between their legs. Well I shall barter such role-playing for many a realistic concession, and whilst retaining my sexuality will be sure to retain a clear brain of my own as well!

(She smiles sweetly at HORATIO who squeezes her hand blissfully unaware.)

SIR FRANCIS: Of course the whole question of worker relations will not be solved by the likes of Mr. Raddles's union - which will have to ferment trouble artificially to justify their existence - but by a new breed of compassionate management, educated into accepting the fact that the provision of welfare for its employees is beneficial to both sides.

ISADORE: Isn't that what they call paternalism?

SIR FRANCIS: *(exploding).* Well what if it is? Dammit all, there's no crime in hoping to be a father to one's workforce.

ELLEN: A Christian sentiment from your father at last, Isadore! It's not to be sneezed at. What is God if not a universal Father?

ISADORE: You can only be a father to children: grown up men resent it.

SIR FRANCIS: *(wagging a fork at her).* I tell you, my girl, your average worker doesn't care two hoots about paternalism: he's quite lazy enough to let his employers, or the state, father and mother him from the cradle to the grave. What really sticks in their craw is the envy of Class. Just as a nigger blames his every misfortune on his colour rather than his own defects, so the worker makes a scapegoat of his class.

HORATIO: And there are those who fear losing their lower-class identity as fiercely as a miser cherishes the gold he refuses to spend - though neither does neither any good.

SIR FRANCIS: I didn't spring from the landed gentry myself. We're a new breed that passes on its trading wealth from generation to generation. The only blue-blood we can aspire to comes by way of your mother's family - and that's so distant and anaemic by now that it's nearer mauve than true blue. My ultimate origins are nearly as lowly as their's, yet they enjoy touching their forelock to me and hating my acumen and prosperity. It's the day of the entrepreneur:-work plus flair: and they resent that they have only the capacity for work. -Not that I deny my share of snobbery. It's a fact, and I'm happy to entertain it. That's why *your* feet are welcome under this table, Horatio.

HORATIO: *(to ISADORE).* Perhaps we can darken the blood's hue again. Money and title are nothing if not incestuous.

(Off-stage a nasty scream curdles the air.)

ELLEN: *(rising).* What was that?

SIR FRANCIS: *(jovial).* Perhaps the bear has added singing to its repertoire! *(They laugh relieved.)* Come friends - let us repair to the drawing-room. *(Aside, more soberly, as the others go ahead of him.)* I'll send observers all the same. There's been a sight too many incidents since the men lost an industry and gained a Raddles. *(Exits.)*

Scene 3

(Back in the woods. Simultaneously. Darkness, relieved only by a shuttered lamp. RADDLES, ISIAH, TERRY and OLIVER, poaching. TERRY has been caught in a man-trap, which has broken and opened his leg, which in turn has covered the others in blood as they claw like conspirators to dig up the trap.)

RADDLES: It's one of those bloody man-traps. Hold on Terry; we'll dig you free. *(TERRY roars in pain.)*

ISIAH: Ken't 'e stop 'is screaming? 'E'll 'ev the wardens on us.

RADDLES: Would you rather we left him?

TERRY: No - no!

RADDLES: We'll not leave yer, lad. But hush your noise as best y'can.

OLIVER: 'Is leg's broken right enough. I ken't see the spring f'blood.

TERRY: Dun't leave me. Oh my God - what'll me mum say? I've bin in trouble afore. Arh-!

OLIVER: *(to ISIAH).* Dig, y'bastard. 'E'll ev to cart the whole lot with 'im.

RADDLES: You've turned the paradox on 'em, Terry boy:- it's animals as 'as set this trap and the civilized man they've caught in it.

OLIVER: And all fer a couple of mangy rabbits and a skinny partridge. *(Hissing.)* Jason! Jason! Where's that bloody dog crept to?

ISIAH: We could git transported fer this.

RADDLES: *(looking at trap).* Some of the best workmanship in the country, perverted by the gentry into contraptions of mutilation.

ISIAH: You should be happy inough:- it gev some poor bastard full employment in the mekin' of it!

RADDLES: Kent you see they corrupt iverything they touch:- craftsman mekin' 'em erotic toys of astonishing complexity? Artists lured into the depiction of pornography? I tell you we must own the wealth of this country before the capitalists divide it into squares for themselves - same as they did the land.

OLIVER: It's coming. I c'n feel the pegs is loose. Ken you drag it with you, Terry? The whole bleedin' issue?

TERRY: *(panting).* Yis, yis - I'll try. Oh - I'll lose me leg. Me mum dun't know I'm ate. Auw - aa, what'll I do? I'll niver git t'work in the morning. Air mum'll kill me.*(Screams.)*

RADDLES: Easy, boy - dun't wan' us all ketched.

ISIAH: I'll stop 'is racket: I'll stuff the netting in his gob.

OLIVER: 'Eathen.

ISIAH: There's no point in us *all* gitting nabbed, is they?

RADDLES: Come on crawl and pull; crawl and pull. *(The lad hauls himself, clinking and sobbing, over the ground.)* If we kin get yer dane t'the pub, we ken see to it proper in the light.

(They half lift, half drag him along. TERRY begins to cry out rhythmically in hysteria.)

OLIVER: It kips ketchin in the undergrowth. 'E's losing an 'ell of a lot of blood.

TERRY: Oh git it off me - please, please. Is'll lose me leg -

ISIAH: Git a move on. These ferrets is nibblin through me pockets.

RADDLES: *(laughing bitterly).* You really are an evil cunt, aren't you?

ISIAH: I could knock im ate. It'ld be a mercy fer 'im, and we could get 'im back quiet.

RADDLES: And we could damage 'is leg irrevocably in the process.

TERRY: I dun't mind. 'It me unconscious: anything but the pain. Oh dear, oh dear! *(Cries piteously.)*

OLIVER: *(at the sound of breaking branches).* Hist! There's something comin'.

(They stop. Noises in the trees.)

ISIAH: *(panicking).* It's the bear! It's smelt the blood.

TERRY: Oh let me die.

RADDLES: Use yer net!

ISIAH: I'm getting' ate ov 'ere!

(He turns to run and falls over TERRY's leg.)

TERRY: Aaiww - ! Me leg - yer' lying on me leg! Oh, Jesus, mek me faint - mum, mum... *(Weeps bitterly.)*

ISIAH: The bear'll eat the lot of us. *(A form crashes through the branches.)*

RADDLES: *(hurling himself on ISIAH).* Give us the net - y'yellow git!

(He throws the net over the emerging figure and finds he has captured a game-warden.)

WARDEN: Help! Thieves!

OLIVER: Christ. You've caught a keeper!

ISIAH: *(leaping up).* Kill the bastard or 'e'll shop us all.

(He thumps at the struggling man with a cudgel. TERRY screams repeatedly in monotonous hysteria.)

RADDLES: *(stopping ISIAH).* Easy, me old duck - you'll ev 'is 'ead in a mush, and air necks in an 'alter.

ISIAH: Leave 'im with the kid; they'll think 'e did it.

RADDLES: You'ld leave a brother, y'scum?

(They fight. OLIVER nurses the lad. - SIR FRANCIS arrives with two game-keepers, carrying torches. The women and HORATIO follow in a group.)

SIR FRANCIS: When thieves fall out! Seize those malefactors. *(The keepers fly at the men, but after a skirmish, during which OLIVER and RADDLES wind the netting round their attackers, the poachers escape.)* Y'muddling fools.

HORATIO: One of them was Raddles, I'll swear it.

ISADORE: You'll not, if you aim to keep my love! The man's a champion.

SIR FRANCIS: Idiot. You look on the devil as some kind of modern Robin Hood. He's an anarchist and a coward. They'll let the lad take the rap and Raddles will have an alibi by midnight.

(The wardens unwrap themselves.)

ISADORE: I'll admit I've a grudging respect for the man. Reform for the masses is never achieved but by violence. There's a certain missionary zeal about him.

SIR FRANCIS: My dear - people aren't anarchists for the good of humanity. They are anarchists because they are in love with anarchy. They prefer the spurious heroism and lack of responsibility to real reform.

WARDEN: *(unwound)* They damn' near beat me 'ead in. I'm a dead man.

SIR FRANCIS: Take charge of the boy. He'll not live to testify if he bleeds much more.

(The keepers drag TERRY up - who is now reduced to moaning.)

ELLEN: And keep his blood off the furnishings.

HORATIO: He's an attractive little thing too. I'll see I'm around when the surgeon strips him.

WARDEN: *(whacking the boy's broken leg with a stick).* Walk, y'vermin. You'll see Australia for this night's work.

TERRY: *(shrieking in agony).* Cunt! Cunt!

SIR FRANCIS: Come, friends, we'll back to the drawing-room while the keepers fetch the law.

ELLEN: I'm getting quite chilled out here.

(All but ISADORE and HORATIO exeunt.)

ISADORE: I can't help hoping Raddles will escape. I'ld like to see him give my father a run for his money. *(Exit.)*

HORATIO: You'ld like to see his prick give you a run for yours! Between the pair of us there'll not be a man on the estate left in innocence after we're married. *(Exit.)*

Scene 4

(The market square at Stone Marston on a bright market-day. Traders are at their business and vociferous for custom. Itinerant peddlers weave through the crowd:- gypsies selling pegs and wooden flowers, hawkers selling song-sheets, sweet-meats, patent medicines, etc. A boxing-booth has a match in progress; animals are being auctioned. Entertainers vie for

favours:- Romany dancer, Punch and Judy tent - barrel-organ music. BARNEY and OTTO enter, performing their publicity routine. EVIE and her mother are shopping.)

EVIE: *(breaking away).* There's Otto doin' 'is antics! *(Joins them.)*

CON: 'Er and that bear. You'll get eaten by the damn' thing one of these days. Be one less mayth for me t'feed. Dun't come crying t'me with nits in yer 'air. Fulla lice they are. *(Mingles with market crowd.)*

EVIE: Why is 'e alwurs dencing?

BARNEY: Well, 'e 'as to earn 'is living, doesn't he? Sayme as your dad's alwurs meking shoes. Otto ken't welt a sole, so 'e 'as t'do what 'e can t'earn 'is bread. Bears tek a bit of feeding.

EVIE: Dun't *you* do no work?

BARNEY: I tek up farm labouring when the seasons is right; but some employers wun't countenance a bear. 'E ken't reap, y'see, or pick tatties.

EVIE: *(laughingly interrupting).* 'E just dances!

BARNEY: 'Tis a wonderful gift. Y'dunt ask a dancer t'pick spuds. *(Confidential.)* 'E used t'dance for the Czar; but the guards were cruel to 'im. Once I attacked a man who was whipping him and gev the scoundrel a good hiding. Otto broke the back of a soldier what tried to stop me, and as he seemed disinclined to leave me for the favour the Czar let me keep him.

EVIE: 'e's almost 'uman, en'e?

BARNEY: *(censorious).* No - oh no. He's a creation in 'is own right. He got 'is nature, and different gods to us. 'En't no creatures act 'uman - they got no cause to be so stupid. *Their* world dun't need no thought - just acceptance and survival. 'Tis silly mankind that flatters itself that animals wish to be 'uman. In their self-idolatry they ken't conceive that anything shouldn't wish to be as *they* are. They think God made them in his image. Now why should God want t'do that? Did he mek the spiders in his image? Or Otto? What does God want a nose for? He dun't need t'smell nothing. What'ld he want teeth for? He dun't need t'chew t'keep alive. What's he want an arse for? What he en't etting he en't passing! No - we made God in *air* image and worship airselves. The Creator is alien.

EVIE: Otto is alien.

BARNEY: *(pleased).* You've got it!

CON: *(reappearing).* What are you filling the child's 'ead with? She should be 'elping her brother look after the twins. Be off with you! *(EVIE scampers off.)* And where were you, in Sir Francis Sedley's copse lest night that y'didn't 'ear poor Terry Govern screaming fer 'elp? That lad's in the town gaol t'day - and 'im with a broken leg, and no more a trespasser than what *you* are.

BARNEY: When the owl screeches the mouse shivers in his hole.

CON: Dun't try yer riddles on me, y'daft old bugger. You think if you act weird and keep a menagerie people'll tek you for a prophet and feed yer. Well just try coming the old soldier when the sergeants ask you who else was with Terry Govern in them woods.

SIR FRANCIS: *(entering, with his family in attendance).* Good morning, Mrs. Bruley. Encouraging our itinerant impresario, I see.

CON: Yes, Sir Francis.

SIR FRANCIS: Your husband is at the factory today?

CON: Yes sir.

SIR FRANCIS: I'm pleased to hear it. His attendance has been erratic of late.

CON: 'Is bronchitis 'as bin troublesome, sir.

SIR FRANCIS: The smell of leather never did one's lungs any harm, ma'am, and with due respect, his ale-house sojourns with the fiery Mr. Raddles till the rheumy hours of the night can hardly be said to improve either his condition or his mind.

ELLEN: You must induce him to inhale the vapours of Friar's Balsam, Mrs. Bruley. It's both efficacious and cheap.

SIR FRANCIS: *(to BARNEY).* I shall miss your terpsichordian entertainment this morning, sir, I fear. I've a young ruffian appearing before me on the bench, taken poaching in me own woods. Didn't hear any of the fracas yourself, I take it?

BARNEY: A bear is a valuable animal, sir. When there are firearms and cudgels arained I keep 'im ait of 'arms way.

SIR FRANCIS: Very wise. Terry Govern wouldn't have a broken leg and the prospect of transportation before him if you were his keeper instead of

Raddles, Barney.

HORATIO: The youngster's an able body on him. It's a pity to see it maimed outside his country's service.

ELLEN: I couldn't touch him; I'm sorry, but I couldn't. I wanted to be charitable, but the blood and smell on him repelled me.

ISADORE: It was noble of him not to reveal the identity of his companions.

SIR FRANCIS: His very silence testifies to their identity. You mustn't give too much credence to working-class solidarity, my dear. People who have nothing like to think they are fellows-in-adversity - till one or other of them has the temerity to obtain more than the another; then the allegiance is terminated.

ISADORE: But someone like Mr. Raddles is helping to educate the workers into a selfless concern for each other's welfare.

HORATIO: Isadore, he is merely exploiting the greed already in them - educating them to expect more from life than is their portion, and thus making them discontented and ready to adopt his own brand of doctrination.

ISADORE: But what's wrong with expecting more from life and those who already have it undeservedly? If all men were equal materially, greed would be bred out of the species altogether in time.

ELLEN: No, no, Miss Impertinent; the deadly sins are inherent in the human soul. Cain had no bad examples to follow - the world being unpopulated, as it were... but it didn't prevent him from coveting his brother's property and respect, and murdering him.

SIR FRANCIS: Personally, I stand open to conviction either way, my dear. But to be of a really free mind you must beware of your mother *and* the Mr. Raddleses of this world. They're people with beliefs, and any person who holds a belief eventually becomes a slave to it. *(Enter RADDLES.)*

RADDLES: Even to the belief that he has none, Sir Francis? - Ladies, sirs, good-morning.

SIR FRANCIS: You're looking somewhat haggard today, Raddles. Up half the night perhaps?

RADDLES: An excess of honest toil, more like.

ELLEN: Indeed, my lady, I hope you have benefited from the knowledge personally.

SIR FRANCIS: Were you in my woods last night? There's a man due in my dock this morning who states you were.

RADDLES: Then he commits perjury. As God is my witness.

SIR FRANCIS: I doubt not that you will have many a witness for your last night's alibi; but I can't think God will be one of 'em. Come along, my friends; we are keeping a man with a broken leg, standing. We must show more compassion than his peers.

ISADORE: I'll keep Barney company a little longer, father. Go on without me.

HORATIO: *(jestingly as they go).* Get Otto to teach her to dance, Barney. Her cerebral nature needs to be softened with the social graces. *(With innuendo.)* It will take a bear to partner that young woman as she lies at the moment.

(Exits with SIR FRANCIS, who gives a curt little bow to the company.)

ELLEN: Do not be too long unaccompanied, Isadore. It is unseemly for a young woman to be abroad alone in a market place. *(Exit.)*

RADDLES: *(bitterly)* To what sort of justice does he go when the rich judge the poor?

ISADORE: Surely it's not his income he will be judging? You must not be rude about my father. His ancestors were common men, just as you are. He is a self-made man.

RADDLES: Aye, and no doubt he's satisfied with his handiwork.

BARNEY: 'Tis only the money that differentiates between men when all's said and done.

RADDLES: When the workers have the sense to unionise, and barter their labour for a fair share of the profits we shall buy justice as lenient as the Lords get.

ISADORE: Shame on you, to want to share the corruption of Lords!

RADDLES: Parity before reform, my gel!

CON: Well I dun't want no jestice. A bigger wage-packet fer my old man'll suit me well inough! Good-day to you all. *(Laughingly departs.)*

BARNEY: I must gew t'my pitch, missy - with your leave.

RADDLES: And I to mine.

ISADORE: *(in surprise).* What? Are you become market trader, then?

RADDLES: I'm to address a workers' meeting. Will you come?

ISADORE: I'll come. But I'll not promise to listen *(Exeunt.)*

Scene 5

(A bower in the garden of Stacey Hall, Stone Marston. Hot afternoon. Enter ISIAH.)

ISIAH: The heat gets at a man; an Raddles' rubbish dun' 'elp. If 'e thinks 'e'll get something out of the gentry with all 'is preaching twaddle more 'an the odd poached rabbit and a Christmas box, 'e's got another think coming. Dun't do t'antagonise 'em. They've got the whip 'and. They'll always be them as gives the orders and them as takes 'em. 'Olding yer 'and over yer 'appeny wun't profit yer. 'Sides, y'ken learn a lot from yer betters. That Isadore now - pretty little thing; a young turkey just ripe f'stuffing. Often see 'er in this nook when I'm doing a few jobs for the gardner. Dun't see me, of course; I keep well 'id behind the hedge; but I see *that* little madam all right - reading her books and clawing at the neck of her dress in this 'ot weather. Thinks nothing of lifting her legs up on the bench and hoisting up her skirts for a bit of cool air. I tell you, what with the tits at the top and the calves at the bottom a man dun't know next where t'put 'is eyes. Sooner she's wed the better. A real Tom-boy. A feller could be strung up by the horn for poking that before it's due. Crickey, she must 'ave read me thoughts; she's coming this way as sweet as if I'd conjured 'er. She's careless with 'er clouts when she dun't know she's being watched. *(Hides. ISADORE enters, lightly clad.)*

ISADORE: Oh, if only I could write as well as Mr. Raddles orates! I'ld be a published author by now. A man could follow such a leader to the ends of the earth, so to what follies could he lead a poor woman! The thrill of shame at being denounced as a rich parasite quite pierces one's breast; I never knew feeling guilty could be so exciting - like a child awaiting punishment from its father, yet glad at the defiance of its misdemeanour. *He* says that we're two nations - one rich and one poor, and that the coming of labour-fed industries will only create another class of profit barons. The idea that working for someone else for a living is an enobling virtue is a myth, invented by capitalists, he says, to ensure a supply of willing labour. Are we really meant to believe that a savage who collects his dinner off the nearest fruit tree is less noble than a hatter who turns himself mad with his own mercury? If the future world is to consist of manufacturers and consumers then all men must be participants in both conditions, inter-relating, and sharing the wealth they create. Working men must be brothers; not greedy to usurp another's task - as this only nurtures discontent between employees to the advantage of the bosses. No - they must be prepared even to withhold their labour, till the want of it evokes its true reward from the employers. *(She leans her crotch against the upright supporting the back of the bench, squirming her body in excitement as her mastabatory movements and the fervour of her recollections inflame her.)* And oh, when he says such things, there's such an ardour in his tone that one would think it were a lover's earnest address; and his eyes light move vividly than a bridegroom's on his wedding night! His loins grow firm and his legs staunch; his chest taut and his aspect so brave that one would cry 'yes - yes!' to whatever creed he engendered. *(She writhes against the post. ISIAH half-rising from his concealment, his own member in his hand, is losing the constraint which prevents him leaping out to ravish her.)* My sailor may win battles against foreigners but Raddles is winning battles within his own nation - every trade a battalion in a revolutionary army which will bring liberty, Equality and Fraternity to these shores without the bloodiness of a French insurrection. He will inspire both sexes with his sweet breath and eloquent tongue and they will put their hands in his and be led to ecstacy!

(Her zeal has reached orgasmic level, and ISIAH's lechery is about to resolve itself in action when HORATIO's voice calls through the garden.)

HORATIO: *(off).* Isadore! Isadore! *(He enters; stops short, half comprehending the girl's flushed embarrassment, but civilly tempering his reaction. ISIAH slinks off through the undergrowth).* Well here is where the creature hides - like a rabbit in its bower; and declaiming poetry! What a learned little thing it is.

ISADORE: I'm recovering from the heat of my journey into town.

HORATIO: Too much collaboration with the peasantry, my dear. You must take care - infections abound wherever common-folk congregate. Market-places, inflamed with vulgar commerce and fairground oratory are particularly rank and contagious - second only to gaols, which is where your father's just been. They had to bind over your little poacher friend. His leg is festering so that he literally as well as figuratively hadn't a leg to stand trial on.

ISADORE: Mr. Raddles will help him. How can a man be accused of stealing a rabbit from the countryside? It can't be owned by my father when God's wild creatures belong to no-one and cross boundaries at will.

HORATIO: My love, the law is not concerned so much as to who actually owns the rabbit as to the fact that the boy was on private land to acquire it; and that does belong to your father.

ISADORE: One day the land will belong to everyone.

HORATIO: That will be a very unfortunate day for your rabbits! *(Haughtily she sweeps out.) That's* from the gospel according to St. Raddles, I'll be bound. If the professional classes aren't to be conquered by the workers' ideals, will our lust for them accomplish the task instead? I falling to my poacher; Isadore to her Raddles? But then, a *man's* lust is occasioned by beauty, and can be found in his own class as in any other; it knows no barriers; whereas such is the sentimentality of a woman that she can be brought to love literally anything - however ugly; and if that object is also sexually gratifying her idolatry will know no bounds. *(He lounges on the bench, idly fingering the post on which ISADORE has pleasured herself.)* Mr. Raddles' workers should try withholding their labour aboard a ship in storm; then they could glare at their masters across the resultant life-raft. There has to be love between men on a ship; they are so small hate or disobedience tears them apart. Your average landlubber cannot conceive the smallness of a fighting vessel - they think of them as sea giants; yet you eat, sleep, sweat and excrete with another man's elbow in your ribs; and when a cannon blows your lover to shreds his blood may well be hurled into your mouth. If war gives nothing else it gives our love passion. *(pause)* Terry Govern now; he'ld make some sailor a sweet companion. Perhaps it's time I turned 'sick-visitor'. *(With a wry smile to us, he drifts off.)*

Scene 6

(The home of the Bruleys later that evening. A cramped room of thread-bare appearance. CON is cutting bread for the evening meal. She lards the top, holding the loaf against her stomach, then cuts a round, sawing the knife towards her in the same position. ARTHUR enters and hangs up his coat, coughing. He is a consumptive, gaunt man; brooding and weak, but bad

tempered.)

CON: I'd given you up.

ARTHUR: Some on us 'as t'work - even on a market day.

CON: At least I knew where you wus when you worked at 'ome.

ARTHUR: No good moaning abait it. Yew were keen inough t'see the beck o'me when Oliver suggested I left 'ome an' joined 'im at the factory.

CON: It took yer long inough. Y'ud niver a'gone atall if that Raddles 'and' a'started 'organising' yer. You'ld do fer 'im what you'ld niver do fer a foreman.

ARTHUR: *(sitting to his meal).* A foreman's on the boss's side; Raddles is on airn. Kent you see the beauty of that to a man what's 'ad nobody on 'is side the whole of 'is werking life?

CON: At least a foreman ken give yer a job. The Raddleses ken only stop yer doin' it. What's wrong with a reg'lar wage packet, I'ld like t'know?

ARTHUR: It's not the sayme. Us'll 'ev no say in air own lives any more. We've sold air freedom for a mess of pottage.

CON: *(sarcastically).* Is that what 'e said? You've sold nothing but yer poverty and insecurity - and you whine abait it. *(Sits to her own meal.)*

ARTHUR: But where's the pride in it, gel, where's the pride? Mekking half a boot on a machine and abandoning it; where at 'ome yer saw it through from the leather to the foot wearing it? And is that what I'm leaving my kids; a lifelong sentence of sticking stiff'ners in a machine-made shoe - from 6a.m till 8 at night?

CON: They'll do it on a full stomach.

ARTHUR: And a board of extortioners'll git bloated from other people's full stomachs.

CON: Yis, let the Raddleses put men ate a'work while wimin 'nd children live off 'is principles. 'E'll git *'is* pay reg'lar from mugs like yew.

ARTHUR: Y'talk like a fewl, woman. Bosses love your sort; cattle fodder fer the Golden Calf. We're Walkin' into a future split into the oppressed and them manipulators what'll tek a century t'walk ate of - and the likes of you is leading the throng.

CON: Oh ay? Raddles is good at findin' phrases fer sheep like you to repeat, enn'e? That's what's narking yew - that you weren't off werk t'gew to 'is...

ARTHUR: ... 'E knows what 'e's takin' abate. World's gotta live by rules, 'e says; there's no civilisation withate rules - and we've gotta get in fast and mek 'em first before other people - rich people, mek 'em for us, like they alwus 'ev done. *(Earnest.)* There must be guide-lines, Con - but who lays 'em dane; God? The clergy? The nobility? It's all t'suit their selves. What's the good a'bringin' kids into the world withate offerin' 'em summat better 'n what we've 'ad t'put up with?

CON: Y'tek inough time maykin' 'em at any rate.

ARTHUR: Yis, God f'give me, I do - jiggin' meself int' some kind of forgetfulness of me own existence, and condemning the next gineration t'the sayme treadmill. Where is Evie, anyway?

CON: Puttin' the twins t'bed. *(He coughs)* She kin gew 'nd git some balsalm fer you efterw'rds t' ease that bloody 'acking. Gits on my nerves.

ARTHUR: Balsam? What the 'ells that?

CON: Y'put it in water and breathe in the vapours with a tale rained yer 'ead. Lady Sedley were tellin' me abate it.

ARTHUR: *(contemptuously).* Ellen Sedley! Thinks she's the lady of the manor. Wants a tale rained *'Er* 'ead - *and* rained 'er bleedin' throat an'all.

CON: Y'll not be told. Shut up and ett yer supper. I need this table t'iron them shirts I've been stitchin'.

ARTHUR: You kin 'eve it all t'y'self. I'm gewing dane t'the "Crain"! Directly.

CON: Oh Yi? Ketchin' up on the latest orders? Raddles's army?

ARTHUR: Sarky, en't y'?

CON: Fat lotta good earning overtime t'throw dane yer gullet. *(As he gets up noisily.)* And who owns the brewery profits? One of the Sedley's? Tell yer Raddles that.

ARTHUR: A commodity's worth its value.

CON: *(scathing).* A commodity! That's all *you* are, Arthur Bruley - t'be used and chuked away, only y'dunt know which side t'sell y'self to.

ARTHUR: I earn a bit of relaxation.

CON: *(rising, getting annoyed).* And what's *my* company? Hard grind?

ARTHUR: *(over the table at her).* You've said it. *(He goes for his coat.)*

CON: And what do *I* earn?, stuck 'ere? *(Pursuing him.)* Sore fingers? Babbies' twaddle? Messed nappies - and your brain phlegm on dirty 'andkerchiefs? Gew and get addled. *(He slams out.)* Sometimes I wish you'ld *all* gew ate - gew ate and niver come back!

(Fade.)

Scene 7

(The woods. Towards evening. Enter OTTO in tutu. He dances. BARNEY enters and takes off the bear's skirt.)

BARNEY: Last night in this neck of the woods, m'lad. There's a market at Wellingborough on Wednesday and folks as is niver seen a bear willing to pay to see one. But then, when did *you* iver see one? What would you mayke of yer own kind, Otto; and what is man that he should deprive you of that right? Who will you love in deprivation of fur and hide? Me? How ken you love a breed whose dominion over you will draw you to extinction? 'Cause we will destroy you, Otto. Ken you see the murder in air eyes? I ken see nothin' in yourn - except passivity and acceptance; even when you snarl; and when I look into their deep, deep emptiness it's as if civilization's niver bin; the aeons drop away and the dinosaurs roam. You carry the primordial stare into the Nineteenth Century and wait for pre-history to return; but we destroyed the dinosaurs and your turn is next. Then airs. To live is to kill.

EVIE: *(entering).* What yer saying to 'im?

BARNEY: I'm thinkin' a marrying 'im orf.

EVIE: Garn! Bears don't marry.

BARNEY: Once you told me bears dun't dance.

EVIE: But if 'e's niver seed another bear, how will 'e know what it is?

BARNEY: A pertinent question, Evie. Will he imitate mankind and slaughter it, thinking it a rival? Has he lived with man so long he thinks 'e is one, like lap-dogs do, and treat it like an animal? Or will he fall into its arms, as water runs to water? You shouldn't be 'ere. It's gitting late.

EVIE: I 'ad to say good-bye to Otto. Me mam sent me fer some Friar's Balsam f'me dad's cough so I sneaked ate 'ere.

BARNEY: Otto will miss you.

EVIE: *(pleased).* D'you think 'e will?

BARNEY: *(without sentimentality).* Who have the likes of us got but the little Evie's of this world?

EVIE: Y'know I told you I were gewin' t'ave a baby-brother?

BARNEY: Are you now? Yis, I remember.

EVIE: I'll tell 'im abate Otto. P'raps buy 'im a toy bear dane the market.

BARNEY: If you ken afford one.

EVIE: We ken't really afford a baby brother! Me mum en't pleased; one more t'feed.

BARNEY: Sir Francis will be. One more to employ.

(OTTO puts his paw up to EVIE.)

EVIE: What's 'e doin'?

BARNEY: He's admiring your pretty ribbon.

EVIE: 'E ken ev it as a gewing away present. *(She takes it off and tries to put it round the bear's neck. Laughs.)* 'E's neck's too big. 'E'll 'ave to 'ave it rained 'is wrist. *(She ties it round. OTTO claps his hands in his 'praying hands' motion.)*

BARNEY: The Russians applaud a demonstration of goodwill - just as we applaud only a demonstration of skill. That subtly exemplifies the superiority of the Russian spirit. You'd best git 'oam nay, afore it's dark.

EVIE: 'Bye, Otto. 'Bye Barney.

BARNEY: *(giving her a squeeze).* Goodbye, little lass. It's bonny t'hold a body what's not fur! When we come beck t'Stone Marston you ken show 'im your brother and we ken show 'im Otto. *(She exits.)* We share a fate, Otto. Wes'll both die childless. Tek up yer things man, and let's make tracks for air last camp as guests of Sir Francis. Guests 'ave the advantage over landlords; they rent the sayme rooms whoever's the owner.

(They pack up their equipment and exeunt. The scene is bare as the light

fades to near-darkness. A while off Evie's voice is heard calling.)

EVIE: *(off).* Uncle Barney! Uncle Barney, I'm lost. Otto, *(Entering.)* Otto! Oh
that trunk gen me sich a start. I'm sure this is where I were afore. But where's
Barney if it were? *(Starting to whimper.)* I dun't like the woods at night, they
look so different. Even yer own back-stairs look different at night; and me
dad'll give me sich a pasting; but I dun't care. As long as I'm 'ome. I want me
mum. *(Clouds blot out the moonlight completely. In the blackness.)* I shen't
scream. Barney'll find me and the bear'll know the way ate, like forest
creatures do. Barney? Ah! What were that agin me arm? Nothin'. A branch.
Ah! *(Crying now.)* Another branch. I'm frightened. I want me mum, I want
me ... Who's that? Come on, I ken 'ear yer breathing. I'll 'old ate me yand. If
it's a friend, tek it, and tek me yome. That's it. I ken feel y'nay; but yer 'and's
s'rough and the nails is long. *(Laughs in a hiccough.)* It's Otto, ennit! It's
Otto. Good boy Tek us 'ome, Otto. Dun't grab me s'rough. You're 'urting. No
- no squeezing. *(Panting.)* Stop it; stop it. Yer breath smells. Dun't be dirty...
dun't molest me - arrgh! 'Elp! Get 'im orf me, Uncle Barney. Dun't 'urt me -
oh it 'urts, it 'urts! *(Starts to scream in gasping pants.)* Dun't kill me - arh -
arh - arh - arh - arh - arh! *(The screams go on till exhaustion. Then silence.
Blackness. Slowly the moon passes behind another cloud and fades again;
but in its brief cold light we have seen the savaged body of EVIE, and to one
side at a distance, the silhouettes of BARNEY and OTTO.)*

Curtain

ACT II Scene 1

*(In the darkness a child's startled cries - ejaculated in staccatoed gasps as
Evie's had been. As the Lights come up ARTHUR is discovered drying his
hands and face, putting on his shirt and lacing his boots in the tiny terrace
house, while CON prepares and serves his morning porridge, before his
departure for work. He looks up at the screams*

ARTHUR: What the 'ells that?

CON: Sayndes like one of Mrs . Blundell's kids 'evving a nightmare.

ARTHUR: There's niver any peace in this ace.

CON: *(dumping viscous porridge into his basin from a saucepan off the hob).*

What *d'you* want peace for? You're niver in the ace long inough t'know one way or the other.

ARTHUR: I 'ev t'gew ate t'work, dun't I? An' I shell be late clockin' on this mornin' an' git docked.

CON: You should think o'that when yer ate 'alf the night.

ARTHUR: 'Ew would *yew* know? You're snorin' yer 'ead off when I git in.

CON: I mostly pretend I am even if I'm not!

ARTHUR: What's that supposed t'mean?

CON: I dun't want n'more o'your beery advances - there's inough brats in this ace withate addin' t'um. *(Suddenly sitting.)* Orrrh!

ARTHUR: What's up nay?

CON: I feel s'sick. Iv'ry *one* I feel sick with. *(Laughing humourlessly.)* D'y rimember when we was courtin' and I said I didn't want t'bring up eight in a room this size, sayme as me mother 'ud? And yew said 'we's'll manage'; and we'ld sit side by side in this poky 'ole, you stitchin' an' me glewing, jist like air parents before us, and gew t'bed too tired t'get up t'anything.

ARTHUR: I've niver forced m'self on yer.

CON: Y'niver 'ad the gew! But wheniver y'did we alwus 'it the target. *(Rising.)* Oh where is that child? *(Calling upstairs.)* Evie, Evie! 'Ev I got t'be reaching me 'eart up before you'll 'elp? *(Bitterly musing.)* It's all broke up nay - you ate, me in.

ARTHUR: We's'll manage.

CON: Oh we's'll manage all right. I shell 'ev eight kids sayme as me own mum, but the... continuity's gone. Ways change, whether we kin cope or not.

ARTHUR: The likes of us niver own air own lives; I'm alwus tellin' yer.

CON: *(sneering).* And Raddles' revolutions'll change all that, I suppose?

(Going to the bottom of the stairs and calling up.) Evie!'Urry y'self up.

Them twins should be dressed by nay, and Arnold's got t'gew dane to the grocer's to welp Mr. Phelpps muck ate the delivery 'orse. *(Returning.)* That child gits as lazy as 'er old man.

ARTHUR: She teks after me with the consumption. It meks yer feel tired.

CON: You were born bloody tired.

ARTHUR: *(sarcastic).* Yi, yi - we all know 'ow 'ard done by you are. You ought t'be dane at The Royal, you ought, in the comic sketches, where every workin' man's a drunk and every wife a screamin' skivvy.

CON: Well *you* gew and call 'er then . I dun't wanna traipse up and dane stairs in my condition.

ARTHUR: *(going to stair door).* Evie! Come dane 'ere 'nd 'elp y'mother. I'm off t'work nay, and I wanna see yer move before I do. *(Turning)* 'Ere, did she bring me that balsam?

CON: *(irritable).* Bal - whadaya on abate? The kid gev it yer last night. 'Ere. Git ate the way; I'll get 'er meself. *(She goes up the stairs. Arthur places his lunch into a box.)*

CON: *(off).* Ah, ah, ah, awh!

ARTHUR: *(calling, unconcerned).* You 'evving a fit, gel?

CON: *(racing down stairs again).* Oh - oh God - I s'l 'ev one in a minute if she dun't turn up.

ARTHUR: Who?

CON: Evie; Evie y'thick oaf, she's gorn. The twins are awake and rawing and Arnold's still flat ate. *(He stares at her, uncomprehendingly.)* Was she dane before you? Is she in the privvy?

ARTHUR: I've been ate there earlier. There's no-one.

CON: She ken't 'ev bin ate all night. It's you, y'drunken sot.

ARTHUR: 'Old on, woman. There's no need t'get demented. She must be rained abates.

CON: It's *you!* When I kem in last night after tekking them shirts to old mother Russell and fained yew gorping yer 'ead orf in that chair, dead t'the wide - I thought she'd bin 'ome with the balsam and you'd sent 'er t'bed.

ARTHUR: I en't sent no bugger t'bed. You'd put 'er there y'self, as far as I know.

CON: *(distressed).* Yis - as far as you know - and that's niver far inough. Y'dunt care what 'appens t'the lot of us. Supping yer wages away with yer new fancy friends - workers' bloody guilds, band of brothers. Band of bloody boozers!

ARTHUR: 'Ere, half-time, half-time.

CON: I should niver a'sent 'er on errands o'yorn, only I thought it'ld do yer good. If I edn't bin stitching me fingers raw for coppers fer you to open Raddles' maith even further, I'd 'a gone meself.

ARTHUR: Well dun't you call *me* no sot. I felt s'bloody bad with me chest I set dane and fell asleep. It's your job t'look efter the kids. You've always said you could do with one less - well nay you've lost one y'not 'appy.

CON: *(sinking down).* Yis, and I'll 'ev a miscarriage with this one if I dun't find 'er.

ARTHUR: Well git rained the neighbours. She ken't 'a gone far. I's'll 'ev t'get t'work; it's gone six nay.

CON: *(hitting him).* Yis; git ate, y'unfeeling brute. I'm gewing over t'Mrs. Blundell's. P'raps she's over there. They've got chickens and rabbits in the back-yard; Evie's always petting them chicks.

ARTHUR: Yis - and bears. *(Bitterly.)* Loves animals, does Evie. She could'a run away with your old man and 'is bear.

CON: Arthur! Dun't say things like that - even as a joke. She could'a done just that. Kids get stolen by gypsies - even nowadays.

ARTHUR: Dun't talk daft.

CON: They do. That old man; 'e could want 'er t'work fer 'em. Or 'e could do smutty things to 'er - Arthur!

ARTHUR: Stop fancying things and git rained Mrs. Blundell's - mayke sure. I must move.

CON: *(sneering).* That's right, git rained to yer next union meeting. You'll 'ev a fine excuse f'being late t'day - you 'ad a mad woman t'teach labour rights to; and fer all y'grand words it'll be "three bags full, sir" to the bosses; and "sorry I'm late, but my little gel got kidnapped during the night. But dun't let it worry yer, sir; it's of no import. I'll mek it up in overtime - if Raddles'll let me!" *(The child's screams re-commence next door.)* Oh my God - that's not 'er, is it?

ARTHUR: 'Course not. Dun't git s'bloody agitated.

CON: Get your precious Raddles t'look fer my kid. She could be lying dead in an alley while you talk politics rained the corpse. *(She starts to weep again.)*

ARTHUR: *(uneasy).* I tell you she's not far.

CON: Under y'nose or in a ditch, she'll always be far from *your* 'ead. *(Cries.)* Men, men! Why ken't they live in the real world and not in their dreams?

ARTHUR: We shall be living on dreams if I git the sack, 'anging abate.

CON: *(screaming).* Then git ate, git ate! Y'might as well for all the 'elp you are.

ARTHUR: *(yelling).* All right! All right! It's like bleeding Bedlam in 'ere.

(He lurches out the front door. CON runs out the back one.)

CON: *(calling as she goes).* Mrs. Blundell! Are yer there? It's air Evie; I ken't find 'er anywhere. Is she with you? Are yer there. Gel? Mrs. Blundell!

(Her shouts mingle with the screams of the disturbed, unseen child's which grow in intensity as the lights fade.)

Scene 2

(The gaol. Terry is lying on a wooden bench, half covered with a filthy blanket. RADDLES, OLIVER and ISIAH are visiting him.)

TERRY: They had to spread hot tar on it, y'see - t'stop it bleeding. It 'urt sommat wicked. Then they put it in splints; nay a bit of the scar that's weeping starting t'fester. I'm frantic I'll lose me leg. I'll niver do a man's job again if I'm forced to 'op rained on a wooden stump; and if I'm gaoled me mum'll starve. She's that mardy with me.

RADDLES: Ease yerself, Terry; she'll not starve. That's what we're uniting for - brothers looking after one another.

TERRY: I'll not testify against any of you - no matter how 'ard I'm pressed.

ISIAH: You'd better not.

TERRY: The Seldeys 'ev bin kind t'me. Several visits, and their own doctor.

OLIVER: Guile, boy - nothing but cunning; they're trying t'loosen y'tongue as to yer confederates.

RADDLES: Self-interest. They'ld rather you were working at one of their benches than rotting in gaol.

TERRY: *(scared).* I'll not do that, will I?

RADDLES: 'Course not, lad.

TERRY: I were always in trouble as a boy - but I got a bit of schooling, along of my mother's uncle 'evving bin a tutor in 'is day.

OLIVER: And it was little inough learnin' 'e 'ad 'imself, though 'e thought 'imself a cut above the rest of us. The less someone 'as of a thing the more they'll mek of it - as will a balding man 'is remain 'air, or a poorly-endowed man 'is prick.

SIR FRANCIS: *(entering).* What - are the malefactors giving themselves into custody voluntarily these days, or are you assembling to ensure the child's silence? *(ELLEN and ISADORE follow him discreetly.)*

RADDLES: There's loyalty between working men, Sir Francis.

SIR FRANCIS: And honour among thieves, eh? Very touching. How's that leg, Terry?

TERRY: Mending, yer honour.

SIR FRANCIS: My wife's brought you some vi'tals. She hates prisons but feels it's her Christian duty to mortify herself; and duty's a bigger spur to the religious than love, I suppose.

ISADORE: Don't belittle mother's charity, father; the motivation's not the point; it's the deed that counts, isn't it, Mr. Raddles?

RADDLES: Indeed yes, ma'am. P'raps the prisons would be a deal emptier if common people weren't forced into crimes by the circumstances wished on 'em by their masters. Breed children into poverty and wretched housing and you breed them into criminality.

SIR FRANCIS: Come, come, Raddles. Do you suppose there are no rogues in the aristocracy? And they have the best environments in Britain. I've known saints in the gutters. Wickedness is inherent in human nature; you'll not breed it out by placing men in palaces and teaching them sedition.

ELLEN: Original Sin's the phrase you're searching to euphemise, Sir Francis; though being a free-thinker you daren't put your tongue to it. You observe it in a child in its crib, and all the preaching in the world won't quench it if virtue's not there at the start.

TERRY: Shall it go hard with me, Sir Francis?

SIR FRANCIS: I'm not the only J.P in the county, Master Govern, but I'll sue the bench for leniency.

ISADORE: Lord and Lady Bountiful.

SIR FRANCIS: *(touchy)*. There's the lad's past misdemeanours to be taken into account, you know. Will you be pushing your schemes for workmen's guilds as a kind of bribery, Raddles?

RADDLES: An inquiry so soon on the heels of your promise of clemency could be interpreted as a kind of bribery, Sir Francis.

SIR FRANCIS: To the devious I suppose that would be the interpretation. The work-force in my factories has the chance now by its own endeavours, to better the very living conditions you're so concerned about; and to cherish discontent in these employees is injurious to the prosperity of the industry and ultimately, the country; so I shall naturally oppose you with all the means at my disposal; but my treatment of this youth isn't conditional on your behaviour.

RADDLES: The industrialization of this land doesn't have a good history to date, sir. Starvation wages and appalling shop-floor conditions may not be *your* personal intentions, but they're the quickest way to profit, and it's up to those of us who are aware of the problems to ensure that your famous prosperity seeps dane to ivery level. We's'l kip within the law, that I'll guarantee.

SIR FRANCIS: Mind you do.

ISADORE: But if the only way to change a bad law is to break it.

ELLEN: Heaven preserve us, child! Will a girl talk politics?

ISADORE: Why not? I have to live under them as well as the men.

ELLEN: *(to husband)*. You see where your liberal notions are leading? If there is no respect for authority within the ruling-classes, can you expect anything else but insurrection from the public at large?

HORATIO: *(entering)*. Am I interrupting a formal debate or just a general wrangle? I was told I'ld find you here, Isadore.

ISADORE: Liar. You thought to find the boy alone. *(Aside to him.)*

HORATIO: *(ignoring the remark).* Doubtless your mother thinks the medical risks involved are subordinate to your moral tuition?

ELLEN: Don't seek to lecture me by insinuation, Horatio. If it's God's will she should catch a contagion she'll have to endure it as an example that the purest of good-will isn't always rewarded benevolently.

SIR FRANCIS: Surely religion needn't be quite so masochistic, dear?

ELLEN: How can we appreciate the misfortunes of others if we don't provide some for ourselves?

SIR FRANCIS: Oh leave that to heaven, m'dear! Come along

OLIVER: Yis, we'd best all be leavin' y'nay, Terry.

ELLEN: *(to the boy).* Pray to the Lord, Terry. Let him answer you by name. They could reduce you to a number in here. *(Abstracted.)* I had a name once. I was young Nelly Fraser before I married Sir Francis. Who was she? Where did I go?... Now I'm Lady Sedley, the fourth of that name. *(Exits.)*

ISADORE: *(to HORATIO).* Well and what do you propose to do with me now that you have found me, sir?

HORATIO: Why nothing that you've a mind against, Miss Suspicion, I'm sure you'll wish to play host to Mr. Raddles in escorting him off the premises, and that will surely pre-empt any wishes of mine. *(She is shepherded out by her father.)*

SIR FRANCIS: We shall see you at luncheon then, Horatio?

HORATIO: Yes sir. Since I'm newly arrived I'll stay on long enough to pass on my advice to our young miscreant. *(Exit SIR FRANCIS.)*

RADDLES: I'm sure you would advise nothing to his harm, sir... Good-day to you. Goodbye, Terry. Kip yer pecker up and we'll stand by you. *(Exuent RADDLES, OLIVER and ISIAH.)*

HORATIO: *(approaching the boy. With meaning).* And better than they stood by you in the woods that fateful night, one trusts, eh, Terry?

TERRY: *(apprehensive).* I'm not sure o' the meaning of that, sir. I were alone.

HORATIO: *(seating himself on the bed).* In adversity we usually are, Terry. Is your enforced leisure weighing heavily on your mind?

TERRY: Sir?

HORATIO: You might allow yourself the impertinence of calling me Horatio in private. We're not too wide of an age and the criminal classes are supposed to practice insubordination, are they not?

TERRY: Sir?

HORATIO: *(sigh).* I brought you a book of poems. You said you liked verses, didn't you?

TERRY: I like lines abate the countryside, sir. I were niver intended t'be in a factory. I'ld rather be a shepherd.

HORATIO: Playing little pipes and dreaming of goddesses amongst the neglected flocks? A proper little Endymion, eh Terry?

TERRY: I dun't foller yer learning, sir. I always hankered after a - a pastoral life; when the land belonged to the people, before the enclosures. Mr. Raddles says ...

HORATIO: *(laying a soothing finger on TERRY'S lips).* ... Mr. Raddles-fiddlesticks, Terry. *(Producing book.)* You'll like these. They're by Cowper.

TERRY: *(happy).* Why I know him, sir. I read 'is first volume. My uncle got a copy, Mr Cowper bein' a local man.

HORATIO: Terry; have you thought about your court appearance?

TERRY: Sir Francis says it could be jist a fine.

HORATIO: It doesn't do to presuppose that the other magistrates will share Sir Francis' leniency. They may have longer memories.

TERRY: *(fearful).* 'Ow d'you mean, sir?

HORATIO: Well it hasn't been just the rabbits in the past, has it Terry? Isiah told me about the matter of the leather pieces that were found at your home last year. It was widely believed that they came from the factory, but this could never be proved.

TERRY: That were just... supposition. Captain Tarlton...

HORATIO: ... And then there was your connection with the sheep-stealing gang.

TERRY: *(terrified)*. But I were only fourteen!

HORATIO: Precisely, Terry. It was only your extreme youth that qualified you for mercy. *(Stroking the boy's hair.)* Now, I'm not trying to frighten you unduly; I'm simply saying that it is as well to be prepared. If the bench should decide to unearth all these unsavoury precedents it might lead to well - committals, and subsequent trials for imprisonment or even transportation.

TERRY: *(distraught)*. Oh, no, sir - surely they wouldn't 'old the past against me?

HORATIO: Now if - and I say 'if' developments transpired for the worst rather than the best, I think I could put a good word in for you.

TERRY: Oh sir, I'ld be that grateful.

HORATIO: Yes, well that's as maybe. The point is, I could perhaps let it be known that you had agreed to take up service life - in preference to forensic punitive measures, and any sentence could thus be commuted in favour of such service.

TERRY: You mean - join the navy?

HORATIO: *(ingenuously)*. It's a thought.

TERRY: But that'ls be as bad as transportation. I'ld be away from 'ome.

HORATIO: Come, come it's not as bad as that. The modern navy is a career, a profession; one is free and has opportunities for advancement, and in the present warring conditions, there's a lot of prestige involved. Authorities love patriotism. It quite blinds them to the faults, or even the identities, of the men fighting in its cause.

TERRY: Well - I dun't know, sir.

HORATIO: Then there's the wonderful comradeship, Terry. Real, close, friends - not factory fodder, cutting a workmate's throat for an extra tuppence. *(Patting his good knee.)* Still - no rush. Just think about it, think about it. How's the old pegleg?

TERRY: *(peeling back blanket)*. A bit mangey, Capt. Tarlton. *(His breeches-leg has been torn to accommodate the splints and bandage. HORATIO squeezes the thigh, testingly, like a doctor.)*

HORATIO: They're fine timbers, Terry. We'll soon get 'em well enough to climb any rigging in the fleet! *(They laugh; the boy somewhat nervously.)* Now try and relax, my child. I'll read you a few of these till you rest, or even sleep. You'ld like that, wouldn't you? *(He opens the poetry book in one hand and lets Terry lean back against his other arm.)*

TERRY: Yis please, Capt. That'ld be soothin'. Like me mother used t'read the books me uncle got us. I miss 'er a bit. But you're very kind. Mayke a person feel they ken rely on yer judgement.

HORATIO: *(smiling).* I'm a born leader, Terry! I'll lead you right. *(Tightens his grip on the shoulders.)* Now this one's about a country-boy comparing a black-bird's freedom to his own lack of it. Close your eyes and listen quietly.

(The lights fade.)

Scene 3

(The bar of a local pub. RADDLES is sitting with OLIVER and ISIAH. Low lighting.)

RADDLES: I'm not saying as you'll iver do away with privileges, Oliver - but we'll 'ev to aim fer a society where privileges arise from merit and not from money and position.

ISIAH: Right. Like the privileges of the Horatio's of this world when it comes to womin in the Isadore Sedley bracket!

RADDLES: A fine-bred woman's bin known t'look at a servant before nay, Isiah. Yer mind's more full of sex than revolution.

OLIVER: But them as 'ev 'ad a revolution - like the froggies - soon build up their own list of privileges. The top jobs and rewards are shared ate by the new elite and they become as contemptuous of the ordinary bloke as the old nobility.

RADDLES: I'm not denying the viciousness of yuman nature , Oliver - but it's up to us to educate the working-classes away from self-interest, in which they're just aping their oppressors, and t'wards community responsibility. And that mean's economical equality to start with. We ken only gew a step at a time. *You* wun't see a time when workers form a government of true democracy, with the lords swep' away neither will I; but we've got t'be prepared to act as stairways, trod by others to reach the pinnacle of self-determination.

ISIAH: There'll always be lords while men crave to be ones.

RADDLES: Exactly: we've got to teach 'em that being a lord is of no account. But yer new lords wun't be gentry. The time is coming when the bourgeoisie will tek their place. Ivery factory and mill owner will be 'is own lord and us'll be back in a feudal system where industrialists are the new rulers; but they'll need *us* t'do it - they'll tek ivery worker ate of 'is own ace and put 'im in a privately owned sweat shop. But it needn't be slavery, cause we ken ride to the top, even with them on air backs - but we've got to mayke it mutual; we've got to unionise and bargain *nay*, or it'll tek 200 years t'break free of the new barons - just as it did with the old.

OLIVER: You'll need the working man represented in Parliament fer that.

RADDLES: Not represented, lad - working men *in* Parliament.

ISIAH: Psha!

RADDLES: It'll come, I tell yer.

OLIVER: You and your stairways!

RADDLES: The middle-classes are already tekking over the reins of power: next in history, it'll be us.

ISIAH: Niver. I'm all fer ate and ate revolution and let the strongest rule. I dun't wanna abolish kings: I wanna *be* one!

RADDLES: *(angrily excited).* The rule of the farm-yard? Envy and emulation before justice?

OLIVER: *(laughing).* Rape and pillage eh, Isiah? More in your line than theory!

ISIAH: Yi! Then it's up t'the manor and up with Isadore's skirts You should see 'ow idleness meks 'em languorous. They could do with a real man - surrainded as they are with mincing brain-hatters.

OLIVER: Oh come, Isiah - they ken't all be bum-boys or they'ld 'ev died ate well afore nay!

RADDLES: Oh stop encouraging 'im and git some more ale in. *(Throws money at ISIAH.)* Three more pints: and I'll want some change.

(ISIAH staggers up and out to the bar.)

OLIVER: *(calling after).* And dun't meddle with that bar-maid!

RADDLES: Yer' frivolous idiots, the lot ov yer.

OLIVER: *(amused).* Not inough idealism for yer, lad? Not inough Radicalism in old Stone Marston for yer? One ken't philosophise *all* the time.

RADDLES: When will the working-class iver know its worth? When will they stop enjoyin' being beasts? No wonder the bosses despise us.

OLIVER: *(wry).* Und jist as air liberators would in the long run, eh? Eh?

(The door is flung open just as ISIAH arrives back with the beer. Standing in the doorway is ARTHUR with the dead EVIE in his arms).

ARTHUR: Bring me the bastards who did this!

(The men rise and the people in the bar crowd round noisily. ISIAH drops the beer flagons in shock.)

OLIVER: God above, man! What - 'ev you got a child there?

ARTHUR: Evie. I fayned 'er at Sedley's woods. Some maniac's molested 'er.

RADDLES: Is she ill?

ARTHUR: She'm morer than ill, y'stupid git - she's dead.

ISIAH: *(pressing forward).* Dead? Let me see 'er. She kent be dead.

RADDLES: *(leading ARTHUR in).* 'Ere, put 'er dane 'ere on the table. There may be summat -

ARTHUR: It's no use, I tell yer! She's murdered. *(Clinging fiercely to the body.)* If I find the cunt what's done this I'll slit 'is bleedin' throat. To interfere with a child - a baby.

RADDLES: Lay 'er dane, lad. Lay 'er dane. It might 'ev bin accidental -

ARTHUR: No!

OLIVER: 'E's right. She's marked summat cruel. It were definitely a sex attack.

ISIAH: 'E' might not 'a killed 'er. She could'a bin left and died of exposure.

(ARTHUR suddenly crumples and lays the body on the table, sinking by its side weeping.)

ARTHUR: We'd bin lookin' for 'er all day. 'Er mother were nearly demented. I didn't think nothin' ov it till t'night - she could 'ev wandered off with friends, kid-like - you know 'ow they are; but when she 'adn't turned up by t'night,

I went alooking. I were drawn to the woods. She always loved it there.

OLIVER: Jesus.

ARTHUR: *(tearful)* I daren't tek 'er 'ome. The wife'll gew mad.

RADDLES: *(to a customer).*Gew and get a constable. *(Exit customer.)* Yew bin t'the law mate?

(ARTHUR shakes his head.)

OLIVER: Look where she's bin scratched 'nd bruised.

ISIAH: It could'a bin the undergrowth and briars, if she were dragged...

RADDLES: *(hissing)* ... Well dun't keep on abate it, y'bloody fool - you'll send the poor bugger barmy. We need a doctor - will somebody fetch a doctor...? there'll be medical evidence to see what she died of...

ARTHUR: *(leaping up in snarling fury).* Bastards! Bleeders. Filthy bleeders, t'fuck a child - *(The others restrain him.)*

RADDLES: Easy, easy Arthur. It'll not bring 'er back.

ARTHUR: I'll see 'em 'anged, whoever it were. Monsters - vile animals -

ISIAH: Animals - that could well'a bin it, in the woods.

ARTHUR: Don't talk daft. Animals! What's wild inough in them woods t'assault a child?

OLIVER: The bear! The old man und the bear.

RADDLES: No. 'E were 'armless inough.

ISIAH: Ay, *'im* mebe - but the bear. You ken't control a beast that size; not if it were in rut.

RADDLES: They could be right, Arthur. There's long weals on 'er that could be claw marks. If it were brute strength the old man might'a bin powerless to stop it.

ARTHUR: I'll 'ev 'em both strung up.

OLIVER: You ken't 'ang a bear!

ARTHUR: I'll 'ev the old 'un castrated, then I'll quarter 'is bear and force the meat dane 'is throat.

RADDLES: You'll 'ev t'find 'em first, mate. Let's get things sorted ate. Oliver, ken you get 'is missus -?

ARTHUR: No - no. I daresn't tell 'er! She'll blayme me - what's t'be dun?

RADDLES: She'll 'ev t'know sooner or later, me old duck.

OLIVER: I'll get *my* wife 'tgew rained to 'er. *(He exits.)*

RADDLES: Arthur, come on, we've got t'get the gel dane t'the surgery. Isiah, stay 'ere und tell the officer where we are.

(ARTHUR, going, lifts up the body and is shepherded out by RADDLES, whilst the hub-bub from the customers surrounds them.)

RADDLES: Dun't worry, lad - 'old up: we'll 'unt the buggers dane if they're t'blame.

(Exeunt.)

Scene 4

(The Sedley home. SIR FRANCIS pacing up and down in front of his fire-place like a caricature of raging land-lord.)

SIR FRANCIS: I'll not have it. If he tries to organise the employees into any form of militancy I'll have him drummed out of the town.

ISADORE: Father, I wish you would stop playing the heavy land owner. We live in an enlightened society - not in the dark ages.

ELLEN: Miss Impertinence, do not cross your father.

ISADORE: I am merely pointing out, ma'am, that we are in the Midlands - not the industrial North. People here still do shoe-work in their own homes, and will continue to do so till we can persuade them it is in their interests to work in a factory. If Mr, Raddles helps to mobilise the work-force and convince them that they can get fair conditions working through him from us, then he will be doing us a service.

SIR FRANCIS: Yes. But what is fair? If I save money in bulk purchase at the tannery for the industry only to have the profit whittled away by incessant wage demands, where's the benefit - either to investors or those who are laid off? A display of humanity is all very well, my girl, and does no-one any harm -least of all one's reputation as a public benefactor; but these people are professional fomentors and their humanitarianism, such as it is, comes a poor second to the political creeds.

ELLEN: Besides, dear, if we're to divide people into two warring factions - the workers and the employers - where's it to all end? We shall be two races, continually at war with ourselves.

ISADORE: All the more reason why the low paid should feel they are co-owners in commercial enterprises.

HORATIO: Provided one can make feel that without it actually being the case... *(they all look at him.)*

SIR FRANCIS: *(to ISADORE).* Poppycock, they already have an invested interest in the business. Statistics prove that the standard of living rises where labour is mechanised and organised. And they can always buy shares in the companies.

ISADORE: *(aside).* Let them eat cake.

SIR FRANCIS: Eh?

ELLEN: The good Lord entreats us all to have due respect for those placed in authority over us.

ISADORE: With all due respects, mama, the good Lord doesn't live in the industrial Midlands.

ELLEN: Then indeed our ministers should see to it that He does! I blame you for this irreligious insolence, Francis. You would have her taught by tutors not subject to the laws of God. You cannot complain if spiritual insubordinates teach insubordination.

HORATIO: Talking of which, will the insubordinate Master Govern be in danger of transportation from the bench, d'you think?

SIR FRANCIS: Great Heavens, no. His record is wild, but despite my daughter's strictures, you will not, sir, I trust, find us soulless in justice.

HORATIO: I feel it may be salutary to the lad's behaviour to promise him some kind of shock, without actually perpetrating in. He has a predilection for physical work and the open-air.

ISADORE: We still have a sizable agrarian community if he's rustically inclined.

HORATIO: ... I was thinking more of the navy. We've a need of men who aren't already hardened criminals or press-ganged reluctants. If he could be given a choice of a service career or the prospect of endless convictions...

SIR FRANCIS: It's a kindly thought, Horatio. I'll think on it. *(HORATIO smiles sweetly. - To Lady ELLEN.)* We dine with the Sears family tonight, ma'am. I hope you have made up your quarrel with the mistress of the house?

ELLEN: The woman is a godless parvenues.

SIR FRANCIS: They both have exceptional business heads, and you will oblige me by keeping religion out of your conversation with them: a subject opposed to civility seconded only by politics. - Our daughter and her intended will also be expected to attend.

ISADORE: *(saucy, as they make their bows)*: If we are bidden we shall be honoured to do so - despite the 'strictures' on constructive conversation! *(Exuent FRANCIS and ELLEN.)* Do you relish being referred to as an intended?

HORATIO: I had fears of being demoted since the proletariat have so commanded your allegiances.

ISADORE: The virility of the renegade male inflames my fancy - within the bounds of propriety - I durst admit; but a girl's fantasy is one thing, the state of matrimony quite another.

HORATIO: You are willing to risk the effete for the securities of Society?

ISADORE: Naturally. A girl of our class may be a wanton in her mind but she must remain a snob where her body and marriage are concerned. Low opinions are not necessarily to be confused with a susceptibility for low alliances. Besides *(Coquettish.)* a man much engaged in naval warfare cannot but possess a modicum of male gallantry.

HORATIO: I am gratified to hear you say so. You shall not find me lacking in passion, though it be found to possess variety...

ISADORE: ... You shock me, but do not surprise me, sir.

HORATIO: You will not find me a... jealous husband, ma'am, should your own domestic voyages produce a tedium which requires the alleviation of boarders. *(She gasps, but he closes with her from behind and clasps her round the waist.)* It will be a good match, Isadore. Your father is a knight only from his services to commerce and industry. My family have come from the nobility and his ability to make money will be as welcome to them as their connections will be to him when he seeks elevation. - It is a situation not unusual in the annals of the ruling families of Britain. *(Exuent.)*

Scene 5

(Wellingborough - a country road leading to town. Baggage and the remains of a fire. OTTO sleeps. Enter BARNEY who gently kicks the bear to wake it. It snarls and claws at the man, but warily.)

BARNEY: Oh, you'd snarl at a man, would you, and curl your lip and show your teeth? How ingrained is instinct! Somewhere in the fluids of the lurking recesses of that diminutive brain the cells of memory still stir, whetting the claws for attack - great - great- great - grandfather' bear's spirit transmuted into chemicals seep from some hidden gland and poisoning the taming, bridging the ages! Yet what prevents you from tearing ate my stomach with your feet? Gratitude? Fear? When did your killer passions become ritual? Do you tolerate me - or have I taken the place of the Great Bear who disposes the herd's leaders when age wanes them? But bears is solitary things, 'en't they? - and I your surrogate, sexless mate. *(He goes to the ash-covered fire and stirs the pot on it.)* It's breakfast and the last of the oats. I'm more then a wife to you! *(He dumps the porridge in a bowl and gives it to the animal, who slops at it.)* I've bint' the stream and weshed meself and got the water for the tea and the oats. Mebe there's berries too - if them tinkers 'evn't took 'em all. I've done my share nay it's your turn. *(Pause. They look at each other.)* We'm as isolated from each ither as if we *were* married! Two flies on the one bit o' dung. Even those gypsies wouldn't let us into their camp last night, nor share their fire with us: and their very donkeys twist their rheumy eyes on us and exude suspicious sweat dane the channels of their staring rib-sockets. Even the outcasts have their outcasts. - What's thet? *(He leaps round, peering into the bushes.)* Thieves and robbers? Diddicoys who'ld steal an old man's gruel t' feed their whelps? - Ah, there it is agen, Otto! Ate with yer talons. *(Calls.)* 'E'll 'ev yer, s'welp me! *(A little ragged girl emerges from the brackens.)* Banshees of hell - it's a whole army ov 'em, Otto. *(Playfully to the child.)* Are you gewing t'kill us nay; or wait for your crone of a mother to witch us with a spell? *(The child giggles and comes forward.)* It's another Little Evie fer us, Otto. Aven't you a one with the ladies! Like the rest of their sex the bigger the beast you are the better they'll be mesmerized. - Would you see 'im dence, young wench? Though it's a mite early and 'e's in a tetchy mood. - *(He takes a stick and prods the unwilling animal into a few ungainly steps.)* Goaded gaiety - merriment without mirth: laughter withate pity. He hops 'cause I 'urt 'is feet and we're happy at our cruelty and call it dencing, to salve the conscience from our viciousness. *(The child dances too, laughing - then makes as if to touch Evie's ribbons on OTTO's wrist. He rears up in anger. The girl gives a short squeal.)* No! You mustn't tek 'is ribbons. They were given 'im by a true-love, who saw some gum ooze from his vacant eye and thought it wus a tear: and iver since 'e's bin in torment to become a man so 'e ken share sich fantasies. *(Suddenly OTTO hurls his head from side to side and roars t the world. The child flees in terror.)* Nay what 'ev y'done? Your despair should be comic, entertainer, not savage. I'll git yer lead. We mun gew t'market like the domestic beasts. Think y'self lucky you come from auctions with yer hide intact. *(He collects up his belongings again as in the former scene, and stamps out the fire. Then he takes the bear's rein, shoulders his burdens and takes his staff. Some sound causes him to start uneasily.).* Hist! The branches are snappin' . Are we in company agen? *(Silence.)* There's a shortage of the morning's bird song that betokens a rival presence. *(Silence. Calling.).* Are you back, Mary? Is the lure of the pelt too strong fer a female brat? *(Silence.)* It's nothin' *(Relaxes.)* jest an old man's head, that fills up the silences with the creaks in his waxy ears. Come along, comrade: we've work t'do and a fair step t'walk afore we do it.*(Four men loom from the ground and surround the couple. RADDLES, OLIVER, ISIAH, ARTHUR. They carry knives and cudgels.)*What oh, gentlemen! 'Ev y'come s'far t'see a man and his bear perform?

ARTHUR: Niver too far to prevent sich a performance as you gev in Sedley's woods three nights ago.

RADDLES: What was yon lass doin' leaving this place jest nay, Barney?

BARNEY: A gypsy's mite. She were frightened by Otto.

OLIVER: A child might 'ev occasion to be frighted by Otto.

BARNEY: Niver in yer life!

ISIAH: Dumb brutes ken grow vicious, Barney. A cur you've kicked arained all yer life will suddenly tek rabies on its fifteenth birthday and put its yellow fangs through yer shins.

BARNEY: I'm sure you've no call to equate a scurrilous dog with a trained performing animal-artiste.

ISIAH: *(as they encroach).* Nature will ate, old man.

BARNEY: *(fiercely into his face).* Ay -that *will* it, Isiah!

OLIVER: Which of you 'es the bestial nature, old feller?

BARNEY: Which of us does not? Man were a beast before 'e were anything else.

ARTHUR: *(grabbing him by the neckerchief and shaking him).* None of yer fir-grained spiel with us. There's mischief done on accaint of one or the other of you, and retribution bears air names.

BARNEY: Mischief?

ISIAH: Foul mischief. Which of you's on 'eat. In rut - with the fires of lust burnin' in 'is loins? so's the musky smell of some carnal bitch bellows it into flames fit to consume whativer stumbles across its path?

OLIVER: Horns, man - 'ev you horns the bear lacks?

(He rips down BARNEY's breeches while the others hold him. He grabs the man's genitals, crushing them with his fist.)

OLIVER: Is there hot blood yet in this shrivelled winter?

BARNEY: *(crying out, more in fear than pain).* What! Do you debase an old man that hasn't heard the voice of sex for a decade? For shame, for shame - you teach an animal what it is to be savaged.

ARTHUR: *(near throttling him).* By Christ, if you've put your dirty old meat near my babe I'll 'ang you up by it. You'll not be so randy by the time I've worked on your wrinkled prunes.

ISIAH: Push the cudgel up 'is arse! Let 'im know a rape.

BARNEY: Marcy from heaven! What 'ev I done that I'm vandalised by louts I thought were friends. Are you in drink when there's none on sale, or in some evil madness when it's not All Hallow's E'en?

ARTHUR: I'll slit you open, like you did her.

BARNEY: Who? Who? In Jesu's name, who 'ev I 'armed that you accost me? I've no money. Give me leave to earn you shell 'ev it e'er sunset but be not murderous thugs withate reason.

ARTHUR: Reason? My reason broke the day you broke my child's body!

BARNEY: Evie 'urt by me? What devil put sich an obscenity in yer 'ead?

ISIAH: She were in your 'aunts: crushed and murdered - and by who else if not by this vagrant and his be'elzeebub?

BARNEY: I niver touched the child. We 'eard a voice but couldn't locate it.

ISIAH: *(striking him).* Liar!

OLIVER: *(striking him).* Liar!

RADDLES: Let the fellow be. Ken't y'see 'e's impotent? He's beyond the strength of ravishment or harm.

ARTHUR: What do you know of sich things? It en't your kid! The incubi and succubi of Satan give man the strength t'sin - 'owever frail.

ISIAH: And might he not, in a frenzy, kill the wench in frustration of his wilting flesh?

OLIVER: Ay - the desire to violate turns to a blood lust when it ken't be consummated. It's one or t'other: else semen or blood.

RADDLES: I'll 'ev no part in violence to the ancient. It's none of 'im.

ARTHUR: *(pitching BARNEY headlong to the ground).* Then tek 'im yerself! If you'll show 'im justice - shew us some law!

ISIAH: If it weren't 'im it's his accomplice -the bear. They've both got the look of guilt.

RADDLES: *(desperate, as the old man gathers his clothes about his privates and huddles in a heap, emitting whimpers).* Was it the bear, Barney? Was it Otto? *(Beseeching.)* The truth, Barney; let's 'ev the truth. An innocent child lies dead, and there's got t'be a culprit. There's got to be a vengeance to expiate sich a crime.

OLIVER: We're not 'ard men, Barney - but this kid's parents 'ev got t'see some form o'retribution.

BARNEY: A bear touch a child? What cess-pits 'ev you got fer minds?

ISIAH: We're not saying the bear is murderous, Barney. Maybe Otto, jest followin' 'is natural instincts to mate with the girl laid on her and suffocated her.

BARNEY: Yumans is the only animals what lie face t'face. Bears maint.

ARTHUR: I'll hear no more sich talk! The bear did it. It's plain 'e quotes Nature t'shield it. The two of 'em in some lewd conspiracy; leading a mite on with speeches and tricks.

(He holds the bear's rein and jerks and shakes it till OTTO rears and howls.)

ISIAH: We'll kill the bear and then the man.

RADDLES: No. The bear, but not the man!

OLIVER: The lass were over fond of it and they took advantage of 'er familiarity.

ISIAH: Stends t'reason y'ken't treat a bear like a man.

BARNEY: *You* ken - you'ld be that cruel!

RADDLES: *(shouting in anguish at the bucking bear).* Otto! Would you do sich a monstrous thing?

ISIAH: Monstrous things do monstrous things. Ken't yer see it growing wild with panic and guilt?

(They surround and poke the animal, who growls and swipes at them with his huge paws.)

BARNEY: Dun't torment 'im. The animal is innocent, I tell you.

OLIVER: Look at 'is claws! No wonder she was mauled.

ISIAH: Yi. Y'could match 'er marks nail fer nail with 'em.

(They beat the bear.)

BARNEY: *(crying out).* Dun't provoke 'im, else you wake a wrath its taken a thaisand years to quell.

ARTHUR: *(panting).* Hear him! Hear him! From 'is very maith he admits the beast is dangerous.

BARNEY: It roars in self-defence. Oh let it be!

OLIVER: It must be slain before it kills agen. It's a kindness to itself.

RADDLES: And to you, Barney. If it's lethal and strikes elsewhere you'll be damned fer 'arbouring it.

BARNEY: *(bitter).* An animal will foller yer t'the ends of the earth withate a belief in its 'ead. It will love you withate stint: it will kill you withate malice. But a man will kill you for no reason than thet you 'ad a different thought in your mind to his. *(They close in on the bear.)* For pity! 'E's yer brother. *I'm* yer brother.!

ISIAH: Yer not a worker: yer not one of us.

BARNEY: We're all working men. If for no other charity ken you not forbear t'slaughter my livelihood?

OLIVER: Mercenary! A tinker to the end!

(OTTO does his "praying" hands trick. They strike the bear.)

BARNEY: Stop -stop! Oh Jesus, who suffered the Roman soldiers to beat Him, shew mercy on a guiltless creature who relearns his lost violence from the sons of men.

ISIAH: *(screeching).* Blasphemy! 'E equates the Lord with this stinkin' hulk of fear and shit.

ARTHUR: *(demented).* you call that guiltless? Look - there be the foam with which her clothes were drenched: there be the feet that dug into her skin: there be the teeth that ripped her neck - and there, oh angels weep - there be her tiny ribbins rained its great paw.

RADDLES: Barney! Is this true? If that be the maid's ribbin I'll hack the fiend meself! *(He leaps at the bear and plunges in the first dagger. The other follow suit.)*

ARTHUR: Dance! Dance nay, y'hangman's carrion.

ALL: Dance! *(They kill the bear.)*

BARNEY: Oh God, what is man that thou art not mindful of him?

(Silently, the men file from OTTO's corpse.)

RADDLES: *(to BARNEY).* A life for a life. It is atoned.

ISIAH: *(kicking old man).* Think yerself lucky it's dead rather than fatherless!

ARTHUR: *(showing his bloody hands).* The stains shall satisfy the Law and gladden a mother's heart. *(Exuent.)*

(BARNEY crawls to a rock, sits, and hauls the dead bear across his lap, like some grotesque Pieta. Fade.)

Scene 6

(The lawn in front of Stacey Hall, some weeks later. Sunshine. Enter HORATIO and TERRY bearing lightly on a stick, his leg is still splinted.)

HORATIO: You see; you're using it now. No pressure: and in a few weeks we'll have you up and down those yard-arms like an attractive monkey.

TERRY: *(pleased and laughing).* Attractive?

HORATIO: *(shrugging).* All right: beautiful.

TERRY: Anyone would be beautiful in comparison with a monkey.

HORATIO: Beauty is only a matter of weights and measures, Terry. Too much flesh or skin in the wrong places; too little hair or teeth in the right ones, and it's gone - puff! Like the perishable commodity it is.- Did your erstwhile companions approve of your choice, as offered in the magistrates' ultimatum?

TERRY: In view of it *bein'* an ultimatum they saw as 'ow I didn't 'ev much choice.

HORATIO: Come now, Terry. I wouldn't want you to believe we coerced you into an insincere decision. It was surely preferable to a life of increasing perversity and the prospect of transportation to the savageries of Australia? You must think of a maritime career as holding great prospects for expansion, both into the legally adventurous life a boy's spirit needs and desires, and in its opportunities for self-advancement and education.

TERRY: I suppose so, sir; but they all had a queer look in their eyes which plainly said I was nay ateside the scope of their lives - and their ability to welp.

HORATIO: Dear me. How gloomy. You must confound them by being of good cheer.

TERRY: That I will, Horatio. You 'ev bin good to me and I'll recompense you.

HORATIO: *(squeezing his arm).* Think nothing of it.

TERRY: Isiah were the strangest. 'E jest leered and nudged at me and kep' laughin' - though 'e said nowt.

HORATIO: People who have no sense of humour will laugh at anything. *(Enter SIR FRANCIS, ELLEN and ISADORE.)* Here are the Sedleys to say goodbye.

SIR FRANCIS: *(welcoming).* Govern! You look fit to be a mariner already.

HORATIO: He'll be chasing the Froggies with the best of us soon.

ISADORE: *(wry).* Yes. See that the leg you saved in gaol isn't lost somewhere else.

TERRY: Thank you for speakin' up for me, Sir Francis.

SIR FRANCIS: It was nothing.

ISADORE: *(malicious).* Indeed it was not.

TERRY: And thank you, Lady Ellen, for your timely words and visits.

ELLEN: *(stiffly).* It was a duty.

ISADORE: We shall be seeing you again before your furlough is over, Horatio?

HORATIO: You will, ma'am. No amount of admirals shall wrest me from your arms longer than necessary.

ELLEN: Curb your imagery, young man.

HORATIO: Once Terry is safely installed at the naval infirmary till he's fit enough to join ship. I shall return to the bosom of the family and complete arrangements for my security within it, in the form of a nuptial contract.

ISADORE: *(curtseying).* Your romantic nature quickens my desires, sir.

ELLEN: For shame!

SIR FRANCIS: *(looking off).* I see you have other well wishers coming to make their farewells.

(Enter RADDLES, OLIVER, ARTHUR and ISIAH).

TERRY: *(turning).* Raddles! Boys - it's good t'see you. *(They exchange greetings and hand shakes.)*

RADDLES: We couldn't let you gew withate Gods-speed. 'Mistresses, sirs.

TERRY: *(to the Sedleys).* Mr Raddles will be looking after me mother until I'm able to send money.

RADDLES: Yis. She'll miss y'sorely, lad; but she'll know any mischief y'git into from nay on will be official.

SIR FRANCIS: I shall be pleased to donate towards her comfort in your absence, Terry.

ELLEN: And she shall not lack my religious ministrations.

TERRY: You are both so kind, I hardly know 'ow t'thank you. *(Wistful.)* It'll be a sad change from the fields to the salt water, but it is more than I deserve and I am grateful for my merciful fortune.

HORATIO: *(slapping him on the back).* You shall have seagulls instead of blackbirds. It'll be a man's life, you'll see.

ARTHUR: *(presenting him with a leather bag).* We made you this, lad. It's to 'old yer shaving kit.

HORATIO: *(touching the boy's cheek).* Why, there's no more than down there at the present!

TERRY: *(sadly).* It will change, sir. The old weights and measures, eh? *(Taking bag.)* Thank you feller's; I shell think on you in its use.

SIR FRANCIS: I hope the leather didn't come from my factory! *(They laugh. ISIAH longer than the rest, and tweaking the lad's arm, to his embarrassment.)*

ELLEN: Come sir, we will see you to the coach. I have some tracts for your perusal along the way. Sailors are unruly and godless company. You will need guidance.

HORATIO: Will he lack it under my patronage, ma'am?

ELLEN: Do not worry, sir. I have some for your guidance as well

(Exeunt TERRY, HORATIO, ELLEN, ARTHUR and ISIAH).

SIR FRANCIS: ... A word in your ear e'er yor departure, Raddles. *(ISADORE loiters nearby. SIR FRANCIS throws a familiar arm around the man's shoulders.)* There is a meeting of the factory directors tomorrow night. It concerns the new boot factory in Northampton. I have requested that you be present - for some of the debate at any rate.

RADDLES: This is a subtle strategy, sir.

SIR FRANCIS: Not at all. Your guidance in the employment of personnel will be most valuable.

RADDLES: I shall put some pointers - if I be allowed.

SIR FRANCIS: You must not look on bosses as inconsiderate men. You will not find them lacking in courtesy.

RADDLES: Good manners are no guide to good intentions.

SIR FRANCIS: You shall bring your long spoon if you find it a prerequisite for supping with the devil. I'm not making you assurances that you needn't be suspicious. Getting to know you will be in the director's self-interest, I don't deny.

RADDLES: But will they heed my counsel?

SIR FRANCIS: At least they'll get a chance of weighing up the opposition if they don't, meeting you! We seek co-operation between management and workers - not the start of a hundred year war if we don't get the association right from the word go.

RADDLES: Amen to that.

SIR FRANCIS: I'm not saying they'll not be patronising, but you'll have their ear and they yours for a period. Let's term it the mutual reconoitering of opposing enemy camps. You'll not be required during the financial part of the debate of course...

RADDLES: I shall accept the invitation; but I hope you won't take it as a sign that I'm appeasable. It's already compromising my standing with the social club to be seen consorting with the bosses.

SIR FRANCIS: It could be a double bluff, of course; has your suspicious mind thought of that? I could be making you conformable by swearing to maintain your independence. *(Smiles at RADDLES querying look.)* One has to be subtle with a man of your complexion. Straight bribery is obviously 'out'.

RADDLES: Very wise. You'ld not expect me to be tamed by favours. If you feed sweeteners to wolves you must expect t'git yer 'and bit.

(He exits. ISADORE joins her father.)

ISADORE: A change of tune rather than a change of heart?

SIR FRANCIS: Co-operation never hurt anyone.

ISADORE: Nor did a crooked deal on power- sharing for less agitation.

SIR FRANCIS: It's less crude than that, Isadore. A man with beliefs has to be persuaded that there are areas where they overlap with those of his contestants. Or he must be convinced that the best way of achieving his beliefs is through the Establishment; in this case, Democracy. All moonshine, of course; democracy by its very nature of majority verdicts effectively buries minority causes; but the rewards of office are great pacifiers of conscience.

ISADORE: Mother's Christianity grew from a minority of visionary men. You like facts - that's one.

SIR FRANCIS: A case in point. Had the Jews made the Apostles rabbis instead of persecuting them the entire movement would have died a natural death! *(Enter ELLEN.)*

ELLEN: Come along you two. Why must you be forever plotting in corners? The coach is leaving and I want us all to be present when Terry goes. *(Strangely intense yet detached.)* It's imperative that he remembers us all as we are now; not for his own sake but for our own. That's our identity, you see - the image other people keep of us. It's only memory that holds us together, isn't it? - we change so from day to day; or we wouldn't know who we are.

(Father and daughter exchange glances but follow LADY ELLEN nonetheless. Exeunt. Fade.)

Scene 7

(Some months later, in the home of the Bruleys. CON is isolated in a light, sitting in a chair and rocking the baby she is holding.)

CON: It's almost as if she'd niver *bin*, sometimes. Do you find that, efter a bereavement? You look arained fer signs thet they existed, but the earth seems to 'ev swallered 'em up -which is jest what it's done, I suppose. End y'kent 'ev momentos abait -not in this kind of ace. Kiddies' dresses 'ev t'gew to the next child as it gets old inough fer't; and the toys gew the sayme way. No pictures neither. We en't well orf inough to 'ev drawings done of relatives - not even them black things... silhouettes, the parsons dote on. I find meself thinkin' but what did you look like, Evie?' and nothing comes in my mind. Any image I conjure up jest gits confused with the other babies. So in a way it's as if she's still with us -though this one turned ate t'be a boy.- Terry Govern's mother says she feels the sayme abate 'im - though 'es alive, fer all we know. -What I kent mayke ate is Arthur's attitude:- 'e's thet quiet. Scarce looks at the child, and almost niver at me. I'm a skivvy and a getter of meals, that's all; and life is one long meal in this ace. Families is one unit when they're at board and no ither time. It's like a daily sacrament -more so 'an the

bedroom, thet's a fact. 'E 'ev 'is factory and 'is so called social meetin's with
their argufying and politics, and I stick linings on vamps at 'ome t'welp ate
with the coppers, though the glue teks me breath away, and iverything seems
normal. But it en't. - One day efter the murder I went in the fields and
'edgerows where she used t'gew and everything was bright and normal and
cheerful: then I saw it. There was this blackbird peckin' at a bit of twig, only
when I looked I saw it were a worm. Natural inough, y'might think. It pulled
it and clawed it and chewed et up t'mek it easier t'swaller; and all the time it
were alive, wriggling in payne; and iverywhere y'looked it were the sayme:-
sommat being killed; spiders suckin' on flies, cats crawnching the 'eads off
birds, owls dissecting mice; and the farmers men slaughterin' pigs and pole-
axing calves. And all on a pleasant sunny day. So nay I ken't abide Nature.
There's some as believe that what is natural is right, but I ken't look at it or
my own life any more withate wonderin' what's gewin' on underneath the
surface; what's dying in the grass or festering in men's hearts; and what death
I'm breeding my babies for - eh, my precious? Suck on mummy. *(She breast
feeds the child.)* D'you think you bite meat when you suck? Feed, feed on
mummy. The glue's waiting for 'er and ateside there's only the night.

(Fade.)

Scene 8

*(Evening in the kitchen of RADDLES cottage. He is seated in a bath in front
of the fire, scrubbing himself. Seated on a chair by him is Sir Francis.)*

SIR FRANCIS: ... So I was wondering if the time hasn't come when you can
gracefully give up leading the men's social club. It's already busying itself
with wages and conditions more than recreation, which is what you planned;
but others can do that as well as you. There's Oliver. If you're going to make
inroads into the future of worker's rights in this country, you've got to come
into the parliamentary fold - politicise yourself. Groups of workers outside the
Law can't effect the changes you want to see. You've got to be inside the
system to change its direction.

RADDLES: Bin puttin' the wind up your board with the men's demands, 'ev I?

SIR FRANCIS: Well -

RADDLES: It isn't always wise to ask a shark t'kill yer pikes for yer. - You
thought to neutralize me by institutionalizing me; that's the top and bottom

of it; but I've not proved malleable inough for yer, 'ev I?

SIR FRANCIS: Oh I shall always be on the side of my shareholders, never fear. I've a duty to them as much as you've a duty to the labourers, and I'll fight you both tooth and nail when our interests clash: but modern industry is partnership. I've got to face facts:- we sink without each other. And you're becoming something of a celebrity in this area:- endless committees, parish councils... There's quite an air of respectability hanging round you these days.

RADDLES: And there's nothing like that for waterin' a man's principles, is they? You're a canny bugger.

SIR FRANCIS: I'm talking about compromise, not renunciation. You're something of a folk-hero too. Ever since the bear the townsfolk look on you as a sort of St. George. It was rough justice - but it was justice all the same, and people like to have their ceremonial sacrifices. I'm not denying I'ld welcome a change of address from you. Anarchy *inside* the parliamentary system is sometimes more effective than outside it; and it would keep you off my daughter's doorstep every time Horatio vacates it. There's been something of a tradition for Radicalism in this neck of the woods and with them joining forces with the Whigs it could make a united opposition to Peel's ideas on Conservatising the Tories.

RADDLES: I'm surprised you're not in politics yerself.

SIR FRANCIS: I'm not a man of convictions, Raddles - not that one needs any to be an M.P.; but I find it hard to disagree with a man as passionately as the party machine requires. I'm equivocal by nature. A fact is a fact and you can deal with it accordingly; but an opinion is only an assertion of faith and leads to dogma. Isadore is a readier candidate for the back benches than I am, and Lady Ellen is better material for a parson's wife than a statesman's .

RADDLES: Her Ladyship is well?

SIR FRANCIS: Her Ladyship contemplates the after-life with an assiduity which makes me wonder if she's long for this one! It's frustrating that so many who take up religion give up people. *(Rising.)* If you go into any form of public life, Raddles, you'll be expected to have a wife: but marriage... *(Shakes his head.)* another irrational faith.

RADDLES: There's some as burn withate it, as St, Paul says.

SIR FRANCIS: So I understand. A lack of passion being one of my characteristics it necessarily follows that it's a vice I cannot behold without that sense of amused incomprehension which is anathema to eroticism. - Did you know there's a child been molested in the town?

RADDLES: I didn't know it, sir. I'm sorry to hear it.

SIR FRANCIS: The girl's a simpleton and unable to describe her assailant with any great adequacy. I suppose a man who fondles children carnally can be pitied, but one that chooses an idiot as insurance against detection has a cunning which forfeits sympathy. I'll wish you a good-evening now and let you get on with your ablutions. *(At door.)* Whilst you're contemplating your navel, think on what I've told you. You've leadership qualities. They cross the class barriers these days.

RADDLES: *(quietly smiling).* They always could.

(The door opens as Sir FRANCIS departs and ISIAH entering almost collides with him.)

SIR FRANCIS: I beg your pardon, sir.

ISIAH: And I yours, Sir Francis. I hadn't thought to see you here.

SIR FRANCIS: It's surprises you? I'm what is called 'slumming', Mr. Trumbold. What you are doing is probably the exact opposite equivalent - the terminology for which escapes me. *(With distaste, he exits.)*

ISIAH: *(coming in).* You'll soon be too grand fer us, with your fancy fraternising.

RADDLES: None of your inverted snobberies here, Isiah. What's yer business?

ISIAH: I've come to scrub yer back! *(Throws flannel at RADDLES neck.)*

RADDLES: Give over, man! What are you after?

ISIAH: Oh? Does a man 'ev t 'ev a reason fer visiting a friend these days? We've gone up a step in the world when a night's poachin' was a bit of innocent recreation.

RADDLES: You're not thinking of... ?

ISIAH: An expedition? No, I'm not: and I ken see you wouldn't want t'pick fleas orf y'new bed-mate. *(Saunters round.)* Will you be visiting the public-house when you've finished fandycksing with yer toilet?

RADDLES: I may jest stroll in that direction. *(Guarded.)*

ISIAH: Y'ld best fall in the midden on yer way there, else y'll be smelling too sweet fer yer old comrades t'recognise you.

RADDLES: I've their business more in hand nay then iver I did smelling of a tanner's yard.

ISIAH: Mebbe. I dursay there's more as ken't thread a needle till they 'old it arm's length.

RADDLES: Shall I see y'there?

ISIAH: If the new serving-gel dun't see me first - I should say you will.

RADDLES: She'll feel you afore she see's you if I know anything abate yer.

ISIAH: *(crouching by tub).* But then, y'dun't know anythin' abate me, do yer? Strange how some folk are anxious t'represent men they know nothin' abate, ennit? We'll jest be numbers and figures to you soon - a statistic you ken quote at one of yer conferences.

RADDLES: *(steadily looking at him).* I'll not lose the common touch, Isiah.

ISIAH: *(rising)* .Y'ken start with the wench at the pub. She'll scrub yer back better than I ken.

RADDLES: You've a deal too much truck with the fair-sex, Isiah.

ISIAH: 'Ev I nay?

RADDLES: You'll be a dirty old man before you're through.

ISIAH: I'll be a *man* - I'll give you that.

RADDLES: There's more t'bein' a man than a desire to copulate.

ISIAH: Mebbe. Mebbe not. But that's what it all boils dane to in the end, dun't it? A hard dick and a place t'put it. You'ld be surprised 'ow a man's reputation rises and falls along with his prick.

RADDLES: There's institutions provided for those as ken't contain their lusts.

ISIAH: D'yer mean church weddings or brothels?

RADDLES: A man'ld be better advised t'use the latter rather than meddle with children, as I've heard 'as 'appened in the tane.

ISIAH: Psha! Gossip distorts sich events. The gels love it in most cases. It's their parents object. It's called rape with the likes of you and me. If one of yer gentry friends fucks the new kitchen maid up at big 'all, it's looked on as one of the master's perks. Class dun't stop at the cut of a man's breeches: it gets inside 'em too.

RADDLES: Are we to envy rich men only their sins?

ISIAH: Perhaps not, but if yer ken't buy God's silence they ken buy people's ears not to listen, that's for sure.

RADDLES: You've already got inough in common with lecherous bosses, Isiah. Give you money and where would you not be? Your own sexual partiality tends towards the younger flesh pots as it is, does it not, brother?

ISIAH: *(shrugging).* Sexual desire is a matter of comparatives.

RADDLES: Is it? That's deep philosophy, considerin' where it comes from.

ISIAH: I mean - a sixteen year old boy nay, smooth skinned and sweet, say: isn't 'e more desirable than a sixty year old woman, gender notwithstanding? Contrariwise, who'ld bugger an old man when there's a pretty female arained?

RADDLES: Providing any of them had the power t'reject or accept you I'ld not deny you the choice. But beneath a certain strength resistance ken be difficult.

ISIAH: But that 'as its attractions too, dun't y'see:- lust allied t'power ken be a heady combination.

RADDLES: Lean dane, lad. I could do with a hand after all.

ISIAH: *(kneeling at the tub).* Right you are, squire -

(RADDLES reaches out and grasps the man by the collar, wringing his head down and near throttling him. ISIAH squeals and squirms.)

RADDLES: *(snarling).* By God, y'scum, if I iver fained ate you were aught t'do with this wench's bein' interfered with I'ld slit yer bleeding throat!

ISIAH: It weren't me - it weren't me! I were with you.

RADDLES: Were yer? When was that? Am I and my labour committees to be alibis for your filthy whore-mongering?

ISIAH: Let me be! You'll choke me.

RADDLES: You niver said a truer word. You talk to me abate smelling, when you come 'ere with the stench of fish and shit on yer middle finger.

ISIAH: I niver 'armed a soul what weren't willin'.

RADDLES: What would an idiot child know of willin' other than the pleasure of her own animal senses? The gospel 'ad mill-stones fer the likes of you. *(Lathering a soapy hand brutally over the man's nose, squashing it into his face.)* Kip yer nose clean, Isiah. Kip yer nose clean. If I thought you'd 'ad anything t'do with little Evie's case and the bear, I'ld. . . . .

ISIAH: *(suddenly defiant)...* You'ld what? *(RADDLES stops. Stares at the man whose neck is still in his fist.)* You'ld what, eh? Come on. - Admit ti the tane that you weren't sich a knight-errant efter all; is that it? Tell yer shoe directors that a man in your workers organisation was a common child molester, eh? That'ld give yer credibility a dent, wouldn't it? Dun't parliamentary candidates and their associates 'ev t'be 'beyond reproach'? 'Ow are you in the respectability stakes these days?

RADDLES: If I 'ed proof dun't expect that my integrity would baulk at turnin' you in.

ISIAH: But do you *want* proof, Mr. Raddles? Do you want my confession? or would you rather gew on harbouring mere suspicions, but glad t'give me the benefit of the date?

RADDLES: *(hurling him across the floor).* Get out of my reach, y'viper! I might as well be 'ung fer murder as fer white-washing one.

ISIAH: *(rising and straightening himself).* Right then. I'll see y'later, dane at the pub. Shall I tell the lad's you'll be in? We've that policy meeting t'morrer, dun't forget. - Tek yer time weshing. My 'ands'll be as clean as yourn when the honours are dished ate. *(Exits.)*

(RADDLES sits immobilised for a long time, staring into space. Then with a might roar he stands upright, naked in the bath. He is a hairy man. He throws his head from side to side in impotent rage at the world, in the same way that OTTO did at the beginning of scene five. As the lights slowly fade, he becomes still, like a wracked statue. Sis Francis strolls on to the side of the scene, Bathed in light which gives him the ethereal quality of one long dead. He addresses is in prosaic speech.)

SIR FRANCIS: Frederick Jonathan Raddles became a Whig M.P in 1828 - under my patronage. I was created a baronet in 1826 for my services to Industry. Isadore and Horatio were married in 1816. Terry Govern was killed in a naval skirmish at the fag-end of the Napoleonic wars, and though, mercifully, I wasn't there to see it - the first Trade Union Congress was held in 1868.

(Blackout)

END

Other NTP Plays by Barry L. Hillman

■   **Till The Devil Be Up**. **2m 2f**

ISBN: 1 84094 102 2 . . . . Fee Code A . . . . .*Type: Play*

When Jessica Graine buys an old village house to escape from her unfaithful husband she is grateful for the friendship of the maid, Gracie, who meets her at the station. Long neglected, the house is spooky and frightening and the two women soon become aware that the place is haunted. Alternating between bravado and panic, the new mistress is reduced to a state of shock as the house's history unfolds and Gracie is done to death; till the appearance of the local police sergeant reveals that the house is not so much haunted by spirits as by the maid and her accomplice who have been squatting unlawfully in the building and aim to repel prospective purchasers with their scary tales. Free of the hoaxers Jessica can now live without the threat of ghosts. Or can she? A chilling Victorian ghost story.